Lisbon Unveiled: The Ultimate 2025 Travel Guide

Discover the Best of Portugal's Enchanting Capital –
Hidden Gems, Must-See Attractions, Local Tips &
Unforgettable Experiences

Carl Snyder

1

COPYRIGHT

TABLE OF CONTENTS

MAP OF LISBON, PORTUGAL

INTRODUCTION

Welcome to Lisbon

Lisbon, the sun-kissed capital of Portugal, is a city that effortlessly blends tradition with modernity. Perched atop seven hills overlooking the majestic Tagus River, Lisbon enchants visitors with its rich history, vibrant culture, and welcoming atmosphere. Whether you are drawn by its iconic yellow trams, the soulful melodies of Fado music, or the aroma of freshly baked pastéis de nata, Lisbon promises an unforgettable experience.

A City Steeped in History and Culture: The city's architectural wonders showcase a blend of Gothic, Baroque, and Manueline styles. In Alfama, the city's oldest district, narrow cobblestone streets lead to centuries-old houses adorned with **azulejos** (traditional Portuguese tiles), while grandiose squares in

Baixa and Chiado reflect Lisbon's post-earthquake reconstruction in the 18th century.

For art lovers, Lisbon is a paradise. The National Museum of Ancient Art houses exquisite Portuguese paintings, while the Berardo Collection Museum showcases contemporary works from artists such as Picasso and Warhol. Street art thrives in neighborhoods like Mouraria and Bairro Alto, where walls become canvases for both local and international artists.

Breathtaking Views and Iconic Landmarks: Lisbon's famous **miradouros** (viewpoints) offer stunning panoramas of the city's terracotta rooftops, the Tagus River, and the iconic **Ponte 25 de Abril** suspension bridge. Among the best viewpoints are:

- Miradouro de Santa Catarina, where locals and travelers gather to watch the sunset.
- Miradouro da Senhora do Monte, the highest viewpoint in the city, offering a 360-degree perspective.
- Elevador de Santa Justa, an ornate, neo-Gothic iron lift that provides sweeping views of downtown Lisbon.

A Foodie's Dream Destination: Lisbon's culinary scene is a delightful fusion of flavors influenced by the Atlantic Ocean and Portugal's colonial past. Seafood lovers will relish fresh **bacalhau** (salted cod), grilled sardines, and succulent octopus dishes. A must-try is the famous **pastel de nata**, a creamy custard tart with a caramelized top, best enjoyed at **Pastéis de Belém**, where the original 19th-century recipe remains a secret.

Food markets like Time Out Market in Cais do Sodré bring together Lisbon's best chefs under one roof, offering a gastronomic journey through Portuguese cuisine. Meanwhile, authentic tasquinhas (local taverns) in Bairro Alto and

Alfama serve hearty, traditional meals accompanied by local wines and Ginjinha, a cherry liqueur beloved by locals.

A City That Never Sleeps: Lisbon's nightlife is as diverse as the city itself. Bairro Alto transforms into a lively open-air party with bars lining the streets, offering everything from craft cocktails to local beer. For a more refined evening, the **Fado houses of Alfama** provide an intimate setting where melancholic Portuguese folk music tells stories of love and longing.

Nightclubs such as Lux Frágil, co-owned by actor John Malkovich, offer world-class DJs and a stylish ambiance, while the riverfront district of Cais do Sodré pulsates with eclectic bars and clubs, making it the heart of Lisbon's late-night scene.

Sun, Sand, and Scenic Escapes: Lisbon is one of the few European capitals with easy access to stunning beaches. A short train ride from the city center leads to **Cascais**, a charming coastal town with golden sands and clear waters. **Praia do Guincho**, known for its strong waves, is a paradise for surfers, while the serene **Costa da Caparica** stretches for miles, offering unspoiled beaches perfect for a relaxing escape.

For nature enthusiasts, Sintra, a UNESCO World Heritage site, is a fairytale destination filled with enchanting palaces, mystical forests, and breathtaking cliffs. Highlights include the colorful Pena Palace, the romantic Quinta da Regaleira, and the rugged beauty of Cabo da Roca, the westernmost point of mainland Europe.

A Budget-Friendly European Gem: Compared to other Western European capitals, Lisbon offers incredible value for travelers. Public transportation is affordable, food is reasonably priced, and many attractions are free or low-cost. Walking through neighborhoods like Alfama, Bairro Alto, and Graça provides authentic experiences without spending a dime. The city's affordability makes it an ideal destination for backpackers, families, and luxury travelers alike.

Warm and Welcoming Locals: Portuguese hospitality is legendary. The people of Lisbon, known as **Lisboetas**, are friendly, helpful, and proud of their city's rich heritage. Whether you're lost in the winding streets of Alfama or seeking restaurant recommendations, locals are always eager to assist. English is widely spoken, especially in tourist areas, making it easy for visitors to communicate and navigate the city.

A City of Endless Discoveries: Lisbon is a city that beckons exploration. Every street corner holds a new surprise, from hidden alleyways adorned with **azulejos** to lively plazas where street musicians perform. Whether you're sipping espresso at a riverside café, getting lost in the labyrinthine streets of Mouraria, or gazing at the Atlantic from the **Torre de Belém**, Lisbon offers an ever-evolving adventure.

With its unique blend of history, culture, gastronomy, and vibrant energy, Lisbon stands as one of the most captivating cities in the world. Once you visit, it's impossible not to fall in love with its charm, making it a destination you'll want to return to again and again.

A Brief History of Lisbon

Origins: A City Older Than Rome: Lisbon's history dates back to at least **3,000 years ago**, making it **one of the oldest cities in Europe**, even predating Rome, London, and Paris. The earliest known settlers were likely **the Phoenicians** around **1200 BCE**, who established a trading post here due to the city's strategic location along the Atlantic coast.

The city's original name, Olisipo, is believed to be derived from Phoenician or pre-Roman Iberian roots, possibly meaning "Safe Harbor." Some legends even claim that Ulysses, the mythical Greek hero, founded the city, linking its name to "Ulisseya."

Roman Rule & Prosperity (205 BCE – 409 CE): Lisbon fell under **Roman control** in **205 BCE**, becoming an important city in the province of **Lusitania**. The Romans built **roads, aqueducts, temples, and amphitheaters**, turning Lisbon into a thriving urban center. It was during this time that the city was officially called **Felicitas Julia**, a name granted by **Julius Caesar** in recognition of its loyalty to Rome.

The Roman influence still lingers in Lisbon today—traces of their civilization can be seen in the ruins of the Roman Theater near the Alfama district, as well as the underground Roman Galleries, which are open to the public only a few days a year.

The Visigothic & Moorish Era (5th – 12th Century): After the fall of the Roman Empire, Lisbon was taken over by the **Visigoths** in the 5th century. However, the most significant cultural and architectural transformation came with the **Moors**, who invaded in **711 CE**.

For over 400 years, Lisbon thrived under Moorish rule, with its narrow streets, tiled courtyards, and intricate designs reflecting the Islamic influence that can still be seen in Alfama and Mouraria today. The Moors introduced advanced irrigation systems, agriculture, and architecture, shaping Lisbon's identity in profound ways.

Lisbon's São Jorge Castle, which dominates the city's skyline, was originally a Moorish fortress before being captured by the Portuguese.

The Christian Reconquest & Birth of Portugal (1147): In 1147, Lisbon was reconquered by King Afonso I (Afonso Henriques), the first King of Portugal, during the Christian Reconquista. With the help of Crusaders, the Portuguese defeated the Moors and established Lisbon as a key stronghold of the new kingdom.

Following the reconquest, Muslims and Jews were allowed to stay, contributing to Lisbon's multicultural identity. Over time, however, non-Christian communities faced persecution, particularly after the establishment of the Portuguese Inquisition in the 16th century.

By 1255, Lisbon was officially declared the capital of Portugal, due to its strategic location and growing economic importance.

The Age of Discoveries (15th – 16th Century): Lisbon's Golden Era: The **15th and 16th centuries** marked Lisbon's transformation into one of the world's **wealthiest cities**. This was the era of **the Age of Discoveries**, when Portugal's explorers set sail from Lisbon to **chart new trade routes and discover lands unknown to Europeans**.

- Prince Henry the Navigator initiated maritime exploration.
- Vasco da Gama sailed from Lisbon in 1497, discovering the sea route to India, securing Portugal's dominance in global trade.

- Ferdinand Magellan, though sailing for Spain, was Portuguese and played a crucial role in the first circumnavigation of the globe.

During this time, Lisbon became a hub of trade, culture, and wealth, with ships bringing spices, gold, silk, and exotic goods from Africa, India, Brazil, and the Far East. Many of Lisbon's grand monuments, including the Jerónimos Monastery and Belém Tower, were built using the wealth from these voyages.

The 1755 Earthquake: A Catastrophe That Shaped the City: Lisbon's **Golden Age** came to a devastating halt on **November 1, 1755**, when one of the most powerful **earthquakes in history** (estimated at **8.5–9.0 magnitude**) struck the city.

- The earthquake caused massive destruction, collapsing buildings, palaces, and churches.
- A tsunami followed, sweeping away the lower parts of the city, including Ribeira and Praça do Comércio.
- Widespread fires raged for days, destroying whatever remained.
- More than 60,000 people perished, and 85% of Lisbon was destroyed.

Following the disaster, Prime Minister Marquês de Pombal took charge of rebuilding the city. He introduced modern urban planning, creating the grid-like streets of the Baixa district, which remains one of Lisbon's most visited areas today.

19th & 20th Century: Revolutions, Dictatorship & Modernization: After centuries of monarchy, Portugal became a **republic in 1910**, ending the rule of King Manuel II.

However, the 20th century saw Portugal under António Salazar's dictatorship (1932-1974). Lisbon, like the rest of the country, remained isolated from Europe, with strict censorship and limited economic growth.

In 1974, the Carnation Revolution—a peaceful military coup—overthrew the dictatorship, restoring democracy. Lisbon emerged as a free and progressive capital, opening up to the world once again.

Modern Lisbon: A City of Revival & Innovation: Since the late **20th century**, Lisbon has reinvented itself as a **global city**, balancing **history with modernity**. It has become a hub for **art, tech, gastronomy, and tourism**, attracting millions of visitors each year.

Notable developments include:

- The hosting of Expo 1998, which revitalized the Parque das Nações area.

The growth of Lisbon as a tech and startup hub, earning it the title "Europe's Silicon Valley."

- A cultural renaissance, with districts like LX Factory and Cais do Sodré embracing creativity and nightlife.

Lisbon at a Glance: Quick Facts & Highlights

A City of History, Culture, and Sunlight: Perched on the westernmost edge of Europe, Lisbon is a city of contrasts—where ancient history meets modern vibrancy, where sun-kissed rooftops glisten under 300 days of sunshine a year, and where every cobbled street whispers stories of explorers, poets, and revolutionaries. As Portugal's capital and largest city, Lisbon is a **melting pot of cultures, flavors, and artistic expressions**, offering an experience that is as **authentic as it is cosmopolitan.**

Nicknamed the "City of Seven Hills", Lisbon's landscape is a scenic rollercoaster of steep streets, sweeping viewpoints, and historic neighborhoods filled with pastel-colored buildings adorned with traditional azulejos (ceramic tiles). With the Tagus River flowing beside it and the Atlantic Ocean just a short drive away, Lisbon is both a gateway to the sea and a cultural treasure trove waiting to be explored.

For travelers, Lisbon offers an irresistible mix of old-world charm and contemporary energy—whether you're strolling through the medieval alleys of Alfama, riding the iconic Tram 28, indulging in a creamy Pastel de Nata, or enjoying a soulful Fado performance in a dimly lit tavern.

Below, we explore Lisbon's most essential highlights, facts, and reasons why this city is a must-visit destination.

Quick Facts About LisbonThe Oldest Capital in Western Europe (After Athens): Lisbon is one of the oldest cities in the world, predating **London, Paris, and Rome** by centuries. It has been continuously inhabited for over **3,000 years**, making it one of Europe's most historically rich capitals. The city was influenced by **Phoenicians, Romans, Moors, and Portuguese explorers**, all of whom left their mark on its culture, architecture, and traditions.

2. Birthplace of the Age of Exploration: Lisbon was the launchpad for the famous **Age of Discovery** in the 15th and 16th centuries, a time when Portuguese explorers, like **Vasco da Gama**, sailed across uncharted waters to discover new lands. The iconic **Belém Tower and Jerónimos Monastery**, both UNESCO World Heritage Sites, are reminders of Portugal's glorious maritime past.

3. Lisbon is Built on Seven Hills: Like Rome, Lisbon is famously built on **seven hills**, which means stunning panoramic viewpoints (**miradouros**) are scattered throughout the city. The most famous include **Miradouro de Santa Catarina, Miradouro da Senhora do Monte, and Miradouro de São Pedro de Alcântara**, offering breathtaking views over the red rooftops, the Tagus River, and the iconic **25 de Abril Bridge**.

4. The City of Tiles (Azulejos): One of the most striking elements of Lisbon's architecture is its **azulejos**—colorful ceramic tiles that decorate facades, walls, and even metro stations. Introduced by the Moors and later perfected by Portuguese artisans, these tiles depict everything from **religious stories to everyday life** and make Lisbon's streets feel like an open-air art gallery.

5. The Iconic Yellow Trams: Lisbon's **Tram 28** is one of the most famous tram rides in the world. The **yellow, vintage Remodelado trams** wind through the city's narrow streets, passing through historic districts like **Alfama, Graça, and Baixa**, providing a nostalgic and scenic way to explore the city.

6. Home to One of Europe's Longest Bridges: The **Vasco da Gama Bridge**, spanning **17.2 km (10.7 miles)** across the Tagus River, is the **longest bridge in Europe**. Named after the famous Portuguese explorer, it was built to connect Lisbon to the southern regions of Portugal.

7. Lisbon's Unique Music(Fado): Declared **UNESCO Intangible Cultural Heritage, Fado music** is the sound of Lisbon's soul. Born in the 19th century in the working-class neighborhoods of **Alfama and Mouraria,** Fado is a deeply melancholic and poetic genre that captures themes of longing, love, and nostalgia. To experience the best Fado performances, head to a traditional **Casa de Fado,** such as **A Baiuca or Clube de Fado.**

8. Lisbon is One of the Sunniest Cities in Europe: Lisbon enjoys more than **300 sunny days a year,** making it one of **Europe's sunniest capitals.** With mild winters and warm summers, it's a perfect year-round destination for travelers looking to escape the cold.

9. A Foodie's Paradise: Lisbon's culinary scene is **heaven for food lovers.** From the world-famous **Pastéis de Nata** (custard tarts) at **Pastéis de Belém** to the traditional **Bacalhau à Brás** (salted cod dish), every meal is a journey into Portuguese flavors. **Time Out Market Lisbon** is a must-visit for tasting a variety of local dishes under one roof.

10. A City of Contrasts: Historic Meets Modern: While Lisbon is deeply rooted in history, it also has a thriving contemporary scene. The **LX Factory,** a former industrial complex turned cultural hub, is filled with trendy restaurants, street art, and creative spaces. The **Parque das Nações** district, home to the futuristic **Vasco da Gama Shopping Center and Oceanarium,** showcases Lisbon's modern side.

Highlights & Must-See Experiences in Lisbon

1. Wander Through Alfama's Narrow Streets: The **Alfama district,** Lisbon's oldest neighborhood, is a **maze of cobbled**

alleys, staircases, and historic buildings. It's the birthplace of **Fado music** and home to iconic sites like **São Jorge Castle and Sé Cathedral.**

2. **Marvel at the Belém District's Landmarks:** The historic **Belém district** is a must-visit for its **UNESCO-listed Jerónimos Monastery, the grand Belém Tower, and the Monument to the Discoveries.** Don't forget to stop by **Pastéis de Belém**, where the original custard tarts have been served since **1837.**

3. **Ride Tram 28 for a Classic Lisbon Experience:** Hop on the vintage **Tram 28** to experience Lisbon like a local. This scenic ride passes through **Alfama, Graça, Chiado, and Bairro Alto**, giving you a **historic tour of the city on wheels**.

4. **Enjoy the View from Lisbon's Best Miradouros:** Some of Lisbon's best viewpoints include:

- Miradouro da Senhora do Monte (highest viewpoint)
- Miradouro de Santa Catarina (great for sunset views)
- Miradouro de São Pedro de Alcântara (perfect for photography)

5. **Experience the Nightlife in Bairro Alto & Cais do Sodré:** Lisbon's nightlife is **lively, diverse, and unforgettable.** Start with a **Ginjinha (cherry liqueur)** in a tiny bar, then explore the vibrant streets of **Bairro Alto**, where bars spill onto the sidewalks. For a trendy scene, head to **Pink Street in Cais do Sodré.**

6. **Explore the Colorful Streets of LX Factory:** A **creative haven for artists, designers, and foodies**, LX Factory is filled with **street art, boutique shops, rooftop bars, and artisanal eateries.** It's one of the **coolest places in Lisbon to explore.**

7. Take a Day Trip to Sintra: Just **40 minutes by train from Lisbon**, Sintra is a fairytale town filled with **palaces, castles, and lush forests.** Visit the breathtaking **Pena Palace, the mystical Quinta da Regaleira**, and the **Moorish Castle.**

Chapter 1

Visa & Entry Requirements for Lisbon, Portugal

Lisbon, the capital of Portugal, is one of the most visited destinations in Europe. Whether you are planning a short city break, a business trip, or an extended stay, understanding visa and entry requirements is essential for a smooth journey. Portugal, as part of the Schengen Area, follows specific visa regulations that vary depending on nationality, purpose of visit, and length of stay.

This guide provides detailed information on who needs a visa, the types of visas available, application processes, and entry requirements for traveling to Lisbon.

1. Portugal's Schengen Visa Policy: Portugal is a member of the **Schengen Agreement**, which allows for **border-free travel** among 27 European countries. A **Schengen Visa** permits short-term stays of up to **90 days within a 180-day period** for tourism, business, or family visits.

Your visa requirements depend on your citizenship and travel purpose.

Who Can Enter Portugal Without a Visa: Many nationalities **do not require a visa** for short stays in Portugal.

- European Union (EU), European Economic Area (EEA), and Swiss citizens can enter Portugal without a visa using only a national ID card or passport. They can stay indefinitely but must register with local authorities after 90 days

- Visa-exempt countries: Nationals from over 60 countries can travel to Portugal visa-free for up to 90 days within a 180-day period. This includes travelers from the United States, Canada, the United Kingdom, Australia, New Zealand, Japan, South Korea, the United Arab Emirates, and Brazil.

Starting in mid-2025, travelers from visa-exempt countries will need to apply for ETIAS (European Travel Information and Authorization System) before entering Portugal.

- Holders of a valid Schengen Visa or Residence Permit can enter Portugal without needing a separate visa.

Who Needs a Visa to Enter Portugal: If your nationality is not on the visa-exempt list, you must apply for a **Schengen Visa** before traveling to Lisbon.

Some of the countries whose citizens require a visa include:

- India
- China
- Pakistan
- Russia
- South Africa
- Philippines
- Nigeria

2. Types of Visas for Portugal

i. Schengen Short-Stay Visa (Type C) – Tourist & Business Visa

- Validity: Allows stays of up to 90 days within a 180-day period.
- Purpose: Tourism, business meetings, family visits, or short-term study programs.
- Multiple Entries: Available as single-entry, double-entry, or multiple-entry visas.
- Where to Apply: At the Portuguese embassy, consulate, or visa application center (such as VFS Global) in your country.

ii. Portugal Long-Stay Visa (Type D) – Work, Study, or Residency

- Validity: More than 90 days, depending on the visa type.
- Purpose:
    o Work Visa – For individuals with a job offer from a Portuguese company.
    o Study Visa – For students enrolled in universities, language courses, or exchange programs.
    o Golden Visa – For investors purchasing property or making financial investments in Portugal.
    o D7 Visa (Passive Income Visa) – For retirees or remote workers with stable passive income.
    o Startup Visa – For entrepreneurs establishing businesses in Portugal.

iii. Airport Transit Visa (Type A): Required for travelers from certain non-Schengen countries who are **transiting through Lisbon Airport** without entering Portugal.

3. How to Apply for a Schengen Visa to Portugal: If you need a **Schengen Visa** to enter Lisbon, follow these steps:

Step 1: Determine Your Visa Type

Choose the appropriate visa category based on your travel purpose (tourism, business, study, or work).

Step 2: Gather the Required Documents

The following documents are typically required for a Schengen Visa to Portugal:

- Completed Schengen Visa application form (available on the embassy's website)
- Valid passport (must be valid for at least 3 months beyond your departure date with at least 2 blank pages)
- Recent passport-sized photos (as per Schengen specifications)
- Travel itinerary & flight reservation (round-trip ticket or flight confirmation)
- Proof of accommodation (hotel booking, Airbnb reservation, or invitation letter from a host)
- Proof of financial means (bank statements for the last 3 months showing sufficient funds)
- Travel insurance (minimum coverage of €30,000 for medical emergencies and repatriation)
- Visa fee payment receipt (€80 for adults, €40 for children aged 6-12, free for children under 6)

Step 3: Submit Your Visa Application

- Schedule an appointment at the Portuguese Embassy/Consulate or a Visa Application Center (e.g., VFS Global, TLS Contact) in your country.
- Attend an in-person interview and provide biometric data (fingerprints and a digital photograph).

Step 4: Visa Processing Time

- Processing usually takes 15-30 days, but it can take longer during peak travel seasons.
- Apply at least 4-6 weeks before your travel date.

4. Entry Requirements & Border Control in Lisbon: When arriving at **Lisbon Portela Airport (LIS)** or any Portuguese land/sea entry point, travelers must present:

- Passport (valid for at least 3 months after departure)
- Schengen Visa (if applicable)
- Return Ticket (to prove you will not overstay)
- Proof of Financial Means (immigration officers may ask for proof of funds)
- Accommodation Details (hotel booking or host's address)

Even with a valid visa, Portuguese immigration officers have the right to refuse entry if they suspect false information or inadequate funds.

5. Portugal ETIAS (Launching in 2025): From **mid-2025**, travelers from **visa-exempt countries** (e.g., the United States, the United Kingdom, Canada, Australia) will need to apply for **ETIAS (European Travel Information and Authorization System)** before entering Portugal.

- ETIAS is NOT a visa but an online authorization similar to the US ESTA system.
- Cost: €7 (free for travelers under 18 or over 70).
- Validity: Up to 3 years for multiple short trips.
- Processing Time: Usually within minutes but recommended at least 3 days before travel.

6. Tips for a Smooth Arrival in Lisbon

- Check visa requirements well in advance.
- Ensure your passport is valid for at least 3-6 months beyond your return date.
- Have printed copies of all required documents for border control.
- Buy travel insurance that covers medical emergencies.
- Respect Portugal's visa rules—overstaying can result in fines or bans on future travel.

By preparing in advance, travelers can ensure a smooth and stress-free entry into Lisbon, allowing them to fully enjoy the city's rich history, vibrant culture, and stunning landscapes.

Best Time to Visit Lisbon

Lisbon, Portugal's sun-kissed capital, is a year-round destination, offering a delightful mix of history, culture, food, and scenic beauty. Whether you're looking for sunny beaches, vibrant festivals, or a quieter cultural escape, there is no bad time to visit Lisbon—only times that better suit your personal travel preferences.

Understanding Lisbon's seasons, weather patterns, peak tourist periods, and special events will help you determine the perfect time to visit. This guide provides an in-depth look at each season, the pros and cons of visiting during different months, and insider tips to make the most of your Lisbon adventure.

Overview: The Best Time to Visit Lisbon Based on Your Interests

- For Warm Weather & Outdoor Activities: Late Spring (April–June) & Early Autumn (September–October)
- For Fewer Crowds & Budget-Friendly Travel: Late Autumn & Winter (November–February)
- For Festivals & Cultural Events: June (Santos Populares) & December (Christmas Markets)
- For Beach Lovers: June–September
- For Photography & Sightseeing: March–May & September–November

Lisbon's Climate: What to Expect Each Season

Lisbon enjoys a Mediterranean climate, meaning mild winters and hot, sunny summers. Here's a breakdown of what each season offers:

Spring (March – May): One of the Best Times to Visit

Weather & Atmosphere

- Temperatures: 12°C – 22°C (54°F – 72°F)
- Rainfall: Light, occasional showers
- Sunshine: 8–10 hours per day

Spring is arguably one of the best times to visit Lisbon. As winter fades, the city awakens with blooming flowers, comfortable temperatures, and longer daylight hours. The weather is perfect for sightseeing, and Lisbon's many parks, gardens, and viewpoints come alive with lush greenery and bright blossoms.

Why Visit in Spring?

- Pleasant Weather: Perfect for outdoor exploration without summer's intense heat.

- Fewer Crowds: Fewer tourists compared to summer, meaning shorter lines at attractions.
- Lower Prices: Flights and accommodation are more affordable than in peak summer months.
- Seasonal Events:
  - Lisbon Fish and Flavors Festival (April): A must for seafood lovers.
  - Semana Santa (Holy Week): Experience beautiful Easter celebrations.

Spring Travel Tips

- Bring a light jacket for cooler evenings.
- Book your trip for late April or May for the best weather and fewer tourists.

Summer (June – August): High Season & Festival Time

Weather & Atmosphere

- Temperatures: 18°C – 30°C (64°F – 86°F), but can feel hotter in the city center
- Rainfall: Very little, nearly 100% sunshine
- Sunshine: 11–12 hours per day

Summer is Lisbon's peak tourist season, attracting visitors from all over the world. The city buzzes with energy, street parties, and long, sun-drenched days. This is the best time for those who love festivals, beach trips, and vibrant nightlife.

Why Visit in Summer?

- Lively Atmosphere: The city is full of life, festives, and celebrations.

- Beach Season: Ideal for enjoying Lisbon's nearby beaches, like Cascais, Costa da Caparica, and Guincho Beach.
- Longest Days: More daylight hours to explore the city.
- Famous Summer Events:
  o Festas de Lisboa (June): One of Lisbon's biggest festivals, celebrating Santo António with street parades, sardine grills, and Fado music.
  o NOS Alive Festival (July): A massive festival featuring international artists.
  o Jazz em Agosto (August): A paradise for jazz lovers.

Downsides of Visiting in Summer

- Higher Prices: Hotels and flights are at their most expensive.
- Big Crowds: Expect long queues at top attractions like Belém Tower and Tram 28.
- Hot Weather: Temperatures can exceed 35°C (95°F), making sightseeing uncomfortable.

Summer Travel Tips

- Book accommodations months in advance due to high demand.
- Plan sightseeing for early mornings or late afternoons to avoid extreme heat.
- If visiting in June, immerse yourself in the Santos Populares Festival—but be prepared for crowded streets and loud parties that last until dawn.

Autumn (September – November): Best for Fewer Crowds & Perfect Weather

Weather & Atmosphere

Temperatures: 14°C – 26°C (57°F – 79°F)

Rainfall: Moderate, increasing towards November

Sunshine: 6–9 hours per day

Autumn is another excellent time to visit Lisbon, especially in September and October, when the summer crowds start to thin out, but the weather remains warm and sunny. By November, Lisbon becomes quieter, making it perfect for a more relaxed and authentic experience.

Why Visit in Autumn?

Great Weather: Similar to spring, with slightly warmer ocean temperatures.

Less Touristy: A great time to visit popular attractions without the summer rush.

Wine Season: Take a day trip to Portugal's wine regions, like Setúbal or Alentejo.

Cultural Highlights:

Lisbon Art & Architecture Triennale (September–October): A must for art lovers.

DocLisboa International Film Festival (October): One of Europe's top documentary festivals.

Autumn Travel Tips

Pack a light sweater or jacket for cooler nights.

If visiting in November, check for indoor attractions like museums on rainy days.

Winter (December – February): A Hidden Gem for Budget Travelers

Weather & Atmosphere

Temperatures: 8°C – 17°C (46°F – 63°F)

Rainfall: Moderate, especially in January

Sunshine: 5–6 hours per day

Lisbon's winters are mild compared to most European capitals, making it a great escape from cold northern climates. While it's the low season, the city retains its charm, with festive decorations, Christmas markets, and cozy cafés.

Why Visit in Winter?

Cheaper Travel Costs: Flights and hotels are at their lowest prices.

Fewer Tourists: Enjoy famous landmarks without the long lines.

Festive Vibes:

Christmas Markets (December): Try traditional Portuguese holiday treats.

New Year's Eve Fireworks: Watch spectacular fireworks over the Tagus River.

Downsides of Visiting in Winter

Unpredictable Rain: Lisbon can be rainy, especially in January.

Shorter Days: Fewer daylight hours for sightseeing.

Winter Travel Tips

Pack a rainproof jacket and comfortable waterproof shoes.

Visit indoor attractions, such as the Calouste Gulbenkian Museum or Lisbon Oceanarium, on rainy days.

Currency, Budgeting & Payment Methods in Lisbon

Understanding the Currency in Lisbon: Portugal, including its capital Lisbon, uses the **Euro (€ / EUR)** as its official currency. Introduced in 2002, the Euro is the common currency of 20 European Union countries, making it convenient for travelers coming from other Eurozone nations. The Euro is available in **banknotes of 5, 10, 20, 50, 100, 200, and 500 euros**, while coins come in **denominations of 1, 2, 5, 10, 20, and 50 cents, as well as 1 and 2 euros**.

Since Portugal is part of the Eurozone, exchange rates fluctuate depending on the global market. Visitors from countries outside the Eurozone should check the current exchange rate before traveling. It's best to compare rates from different sources such as banks, currency exchange offices, and online financial platforms to ensure a fair exchange rate.

For travelers from the United States, the United Kingdom, or other non-Euro countries, exchanging money before departure can be a good option to avoid excessive fees upon arrival. However, currency exchange in Lisbon is widely available, and many travelers rely on ATMs and credit cards for most transactions.

Best Payment Methods in Lisbon: Lisbon is a modern European capital where multiple forms of payment are accepted, but some traditional establishments may still prefer cash. It's best to carry a mix of **cash, credit/debit cards, and digital payment options** to ensure smooth transactions throughout your stay.

Cash (Euros): While Lisbon is generally **card-friendly**, it's still advisable to carry some cash, particularly for **small purchases, tipping, local markets, and transport tickets**. Many small businesses, especially in older neighborhoods like **Alfama and Mouraria**, prefer cash over cards.

ATMs (Multibanco) are widely available across the city, making it easy to withdraw euros when needed. However, some ATMs operated by third-party services (such as Euronet ATMs) often charge higher fees and poor exchange rates. To avoid unnecessary charges, always look for official bank-operated ATMs.

Tips for using cash in Lisbon:

Always have small denominations (€5, €10, €20) as some places may not accept larger bills.

Avoid exchanging currency at airports or tourist-heavy areas, as rates are often unfavorable.

If withdrawing cash, check if your home bank has partner banks in Portugal to minimize withdrawal fees.

Credit & Debit Cards: Most establishments in Lisbon accept **Visa, Mastercard, and Maestro cards**, though American Express may not be widely accepted outside major hotels and upscale restaurants. Credit and debit cards are convenient for **restaurants,** shopping, and major attractions, and they often offer **better exchange rates** compared to currency exchange offices.

Things to keep in mind when using cards in Lisbon:

Some small businesses and taxis only accept cash, so always have backup euros.

When paying by card, choose to be charged in euros, as selecting your home currency often results in a poor exchange rate.

Contactless payments are widely accepted, making quick transactions easier.

Mobile & Digital Payments: Lisbon is increasingly **embracing digital payment methods**, and most businesses accept contactless payments via smartphones and wearables.

The most common digital payment methods include:

Apple Pay & Google Pay – Widely accepted in supermarkets, restaurants, and shops.

MB Way – A Portuguese mobile payment system linked to local banks, useful if you have a Portuguese bank account.

PayPal – Sometimes accepted for online bookings but not commonly used in physical stores.

For visitors who prefer cashless transactions, Apple Pay and Google Pay provide a seamless and secure way to pay without needing physical cards.

Traveler's Checks: Traveler's checks are largely **obsolete in Portugal**. Very few places accept them, and banks charge high fees for cashing them. It's best to rely on **cash, cards, and digital payments** instead.

Health & Safety Tips for Traveling in Lisbon

Lisbon is one of the safest and most welcoming cities in Europe, known for its friendly locals, low crime rates, and a strong healthcare system. However, like any major city, it is essential to be prepared, take precautions, and stay informed to ensure a smooth and safe trip. From understanding Portugal's healthcare system to avoiding common scams and staying safe in crowded areas, this guide provides all the necessary health and safety tips for a hassle-free visit to Lisbon.

Health Tips for Travelers in Lisbon

1. Understanding Portugal's Healthcare System: Portugal has a well-developed healthcare system, consisting of both public and private facilities. The public healthcare system, known as Serviço Nacional de Saúde (SNS), provides affordable care for residents and European Union (EU) citizens with a European Health Insurance Card (EHIC). However, for non-EU travelers, private

healthcare facilities are often a better option due to shorter wait times and English-speaking staff.

Public hospitals offer quality care but can have long wait times, especially in emergency rooms.

Private hospitals and clinics provide faster service and English-speaking doctors, but the costs are higher.

Pharmacies (Farmácias) are widely available, with trained pharmacists who can offer advice and over-the-counter medications.

For minor illnesses, visiting a pharmacy is often the best option. Pharmacists in Portugal can provide medications and guidance without requiring a doctor's prescription for many common health concerns.

2. Travel Insurance: A Must for All Visitors: Regardless of how healthy you are, unexpected medical emergencies can happen. Travel insurance that covers **medical expenses, emergency evacuation, trip cancellations, and lost luggage** is highly recommended. For non-EU travelers, medical treatment in private hospitals can be costly, and without insurance, even a minor hospital visit can lead to significant expenses.

When purchasing travel insurance, ensure that it covers:

Medical emergencies, hospital stays, and doctor visits.

Emergency evacuation and repatriation.

Coverage for pre-existing conditions (if applicable).

COVID-19-related expenses, including testing and quarantine costs if required.

3. Pharmacies and Access to Medication: Pharmacies are easy to find in Lisbon, often marked by a **green cross** sign. Many are open **from 9 AM to 7 PM**, with some closing for lunch. However, **24-hour pharmacies** (Farmácias de Serviço) rotate daily and can be found through online directories or by checking pharmacy windows for the nearest open location.

Common medications, such as pain relievers, antihistamines, and cold medicine, are available over the counter.

Prescription medication must be obtained from a doctor, but pharmacists can assist in minor health issues.

Sun protection is important due to Lisbon's strong sun. Sunscreen is available at pharmacies and supermarkets.

Motion sickness pills may be useful if planning boat tours along the Tagus River or a trip to Sintra's winding roads.

4. Dealing with Lisbon's Climate: Heat and Hydration: Lisbon enjoys a **Mediterranean climate**, with hot summers and mild winters. While the warm weather is one of the city's biggest attractions, it can also pose health risks if travelers are not careful.

In the summer months (June to September), temperatures can reach over 30°C (86°F), making dehydration and heat exhaustion concerns.

Drink plenty of water. Tap water in Lisbon is safe to drink, and carrying a reusable bottle can save money and reduce plastic waste.

Avoid direct sun exposure during peak hours (12 PM - 3 PM).

Wear sunscreen, sunglasses, and a hat, especially when exploring outdoor attractions.

During the winter months (December to February), Lisbon remains relatively mild, but occasional rain and colder evenings mean travelers should pack appropriately. Layered clothing is best for adjusting to different temperatures throughout the day.

5. Food and Water Safety: Lisbon is known for its **delicious and fresh cuisine**, from seafood dishes like **Bacalhau à Brás** to the iconic **Pastel de Nata**. While food hygiene standards are generally high, travelers should take a few precautions:

Stick to busy restaurants and cafés, as they tend to have fresher ingredients.

Try street food in popular and reputable places, but avoid anything that has been sitting out for too long.

Wash fruits and vegetables before consuming.

If you have food allergies, learn basic Portuguese phrases to communicate your dietary needs. Many restaurants accommodate allergies, but it is always best to double-check.

Water in Lisbon is safe to drink, and there is no need to buy bottled water unless you prefer it. Many restaurants serve filtered tap water upon request.

6. COVID-19 and Other Health Considerations: While the COVID-19 pandemic has significantly declined, it is still advisable to follow any **updated health regulations** regarding masks, vaccinations, and testing. Hand sanitizers are widely available, and many public places continue to maintain hygiene measures.

Travelers should check **Portugal's latest health advisories** before arriving.

Safety Tips for Travelers in Lisbon

1. General Safety: A Low-Crime City with Common Scams Lisbon is one of the safest capitals in Europe, with a low crime rate and a welcoming atmosphere. However, petty crimes such as pickpocketing do occur, especially in tourist-heavy areas like:

- Tram 28 (Public Transportation) – A prime spot for pickpockets due to crowded conditions.
- Baixa, Rossio, and Alfama – Popular areas where tourists are often distracted.
- Markets and shopping districts – Places where valuables should be kept secure.

To stay safe:

- Keep your wallet, phone, and passport in a secure place (not in your back pocket).
- Use a cross-body bag with a zipper.
- Be cautious when approached by overly friendly strangers, especially those offering assistance with "broken" ATMs, petition signings, or bracelet gifts.

2. Avoiding Common Tourist Scams: While Lisbon is not known for aggressive scams, a few common ones include:

- Fake petitions – Scammers, often pretending to be deaf or disabled, ask tourists to sign petitions and then demand a donation.
- Friendship bracelets or "gifts" – Street vendors place a bracelet on your wrist and then demand money.
- Overcharging taxis – Always insist on using the meter or use ride-hailing apps like Uber or Bolt.

By being aware of these tactics, travelers can easily avoid falling victim to them.

3. Public Transportation Safety: Lisbon has an **efficient and affordable** public transportation system, including metros, buses, trams, and ferries. However, certain safety measures should be followed:

- Be aware of pickpockets on crowded trams and metro stations.
- Avoid displaying valuables when using public transport.
- If using taxis, confirm that the meter is running or pre-arrange fares for long trips.
- Ride-sharing services like Uber, Bolt, and FreeNow are generally safer and often cheaper than taxis.

4. Solo Traveler and Night Safety: Lisbon is **one of the safest cities for solo travelers**, including women traveling alone. However, some precautions should still be taken:

- Avoid walking in poorly lit or deserted streets late at night, especially in Alfama or Bairro Alto.
- In nightlife areas, keep an eye on your drink to avoid drink spiking.
- Let someone know your location when using ride-hailing apps at night.

By following these health and safety tips, travelers can enjoy Lisbon with confidence, knowing they are well-prepared for any situation.

Emergency Contacts & Useful Apps

When traveling to a new city, especially a foreign capital like Lisbon, it is important to have access to reliable emergency contacts and useful mobile applications that can make your trip smoother, safer, and more enjoyable. From police and medical services to apps that help with navigation, public transport, and translation, being prepared ensures a stress-free experience in Portugal's capital.

This chapter provides a comprehensive guide to essential emergency numbers and digital tools that can help travelers stay safe, find their way, and communicate effectively while exploring Lisbon.

Emergency Contacts in Lisbon

Portugal has a **well-functioning emergency response system**, and Lisbon, as the capital, offers **efficient and accessible services** for both locals and visitors. The emergency numbers in Portugal are standardized across the European Union, making them familiar to many travelers.

1. General Emergency Number(112): The **universal emergency number in Portugal** is **112**. This number connects you to **ambulance services, police, and the fire department**. It is toll-free and can be dialed from any phone, including foreign SIM

cards, without the need for an area code. The operator will assess the situation and direct your call to the relevant service.

If you require an ambulance, press 1 when prompted.

For police assistance, press 2.

If there is a fire emergency, remain on the line and provide details.

The 112 service is multilingual, meaning operators can assist in English, Portuguese, Spanish, and sometimes French or German, making it accessible for international visitors.

2. Local Police Contacts: While **112** is the fastest way to reach the police, Lisbon has several local police stations where travelers can report non-emergency issues such as **theft, lost belongings, or suspicious activity**.

Lisbon Metropolitan Police (PSP – Polícia de Segurança Pública)

General Contact: +351 213 422 222

Nearest police station: Rua da Palma 31, 1150-278 Lisboa

Services: Tourist assistance, lost property reports, and general security concerns

Tourist Police (Polícia do Turismo)

Contact: +351 217 654 242

Location: Praça dos Restauradores, 1250-188 Lisboa

Specially trained officers assist tourists with lost passports, minor crimes, and safety concerns.

3. Medical Emergencies & Hospitals: Lisbon has a well-developed healthcare system with **public hospitals, private clinics, and 24-hour emergency services.** If you require urgent medical care, dial **112** and ask for an ambulance, or go to the nearest hospital with an emergency unit (**Urgências**).

Santa Maria Hospital (Hospital de Santa Maria) – Public Hospital

Contact: +351 217 805 000

Address: Av. Prof. Egas Moniz, 1649-035 Lisboa

One of Lisbon's largest hospitals, with a 24-hour emergency unit.

São José Hospital (Hospital de São José) – Public Hospital

Contact: +351 218 841 000

Address: Rua José António Serrano, 1150-199 Lisboa

Specializes in trauma care and emergency treatment.

Hospital da Luz Lisboa – Private Hospital

Contact: +351 217 104 400

Address: Av. Lusíada 100, 1500-650 Lisboa

A high-end private hospital with English-speaking staff.

4. Pharmacies & Emergency Pharmacies: Pharmacies (**Farmácias**) in Lisbon are well-stocked and often have English-speaking staff. Regular pharmacies operate from **9 AM to 7 PM**, but **24-hour pharmacies** rotate across the city.

To find a 24-hour pharmacy, visit the official Portuguese pharmacy website: www.farmaciasdeservico.net

Farmácia Sá da Bandeira (24-Hour Service)

Contact: +351 213 420 166

Address: Rua da Conceição 55, 1100-158 Lisboa

5. Embassy Contacts: If you need assistance with lost passports, legal issues, or travel documents, your country's embassy can provide assistance. Some key embassies in Lisbon include:

U.S. Embassy in Lisbon

Contact: +351 217 273 300

Address: Avenida das Forças Armadas, 133C, 1600-081 Lisboa

British Embassy

Contact: +351 213 924 000

Address: Rua de São Bernardo 33, 1249-082 Lisboa

Canadian Embassy

Contact: +351 213 164 600

Address: Avenida da Liberdade 196-200 3rd Flloor, 1269-121 Lisboa

If your country's embassy is not listed, check the official embassy directory or your government's travel website before visiting Portugal.

Useful Apps for Travelers in Lisbon

Technology can make travel more convenient and stress-free, and Lisbon offers a range of apps that help with transportation, navigation, dining, language translation, and emergency assistance. Below are some of the most essential apps for travelers.

1. Transportation & Navigation Apps

- Google Maps (iOS / Android)
  - The best tool for real-time navigation, public transport routes, and walking directions.
  - Offline maps can be downloaded for areas with poor network coverage.
- Carris App (iOS / Android)
  - Lisbon's official public transport app for buses, trams, and funiculars.
  - Shows real-time arrivals, routes, and service disruptions.
- Bolt / Uber (iOS / Android)
  - Ridesharing services available throughout Lisbon, often cheaper than taxis.
- Metro Lisboa (iOS / Android)
  - Provides metro maps, timetables, and ticketing information.

2. Language & Translation Apps

- Google Translate (iOS / Android)

o Essential for translating menus, signs, and basic Portuguese phrases.
o Offers voice translation and offline language packs.

- Duolingo (iOS / Android)

  o A fun app for learning basic Portuguese before or during your trip.

3. Dining & Food Apps

- Zomato (iOS / Android)

  o Helps find the best restaurants, cafes, and bars with user reviews and menus.

- TheFork (iOS / Android)

  o Allows users to book tables and get discounts at Lisbon restaurants.

4. Emergency & Health Apps

- SNS 24 App (iOS / Android)

  o Portugal's National Health Service app, useful for finding medical clinics and pharmacies.

- Red Cross First Aid App (iOS / Android)

  o Provides first aid tips for handling minor injuries and emergencies.

5. Currency & Budgeting Apps

- XE Currency (iOS / Android)

  o Offers real-time currency exchange rates and currency conversion.

- Revolut / Wise (iOS / Android)
    - Digital banking apps that offer low-cost foreign exchange and contactless payments.

By keeping these essential emergency contacts and useful apps handy, your Lisbon trip will be safer, smoother, and more enjoyable. Whether navigating the city, dining at top restaurants, or handling an emergency, being well-prepared ensures a worry-free experience in Portugal's charming capital.

Chapter 2

Arriving in Lisbon: Airports & Transportation

Lisbon, the vibrant and historic capital of Portugal, is a well-connected city that serves as a major gateway to Europe and beyond. Whether you are arriving from another country or traveling domestically, Lisbon's transportation network makes it easy to reach and navigate the city.

The city's primary entry point is Humberto Delgado Airport (Lisbon Airport), which welcomes millions of passengers annually. Upon arrival, visitors have several convenient transport options to reach the city center and their accommodations. In this chapter, we explore everything you need to know about arriving in Lisbon, from airport services to transportation options, ensuring a smooth and stress-free start to your trip.

1. Lisbon Humberto Delgado Airport (LIS)
Overview

Lisbon's Humberto Delgado Airport (LIS), commonly referred to as Lisbon Airport, is Portugal's busiest airport and one of the largest in Southern Europe. It handles both international and domestic flights, making it a key hub for travelers from around the world.

- IATA Code: LIS
- Location: About 7 km (4.3 miles) north of Lisbon's city center
- Terminals: Two terminals (Terminal 1 & Terminal 2)

- Airlines: Major carriers include TAP Air Portugal, Ryanair, easyJet, Lufthansa, British Airways, Emirates, Air France, and many more.
- Annual Passenger Traffic: Over 30 million passengers per year

Airport Terminals & Facilities

Lisbon Airport consists of two terminals, each serving different types of flights:

- Terminal 1 (T1): The main terminal, handling most international and domestic flights. It has a wide range of services, including duty-free shops, restaurants, baggage claim, currency exchange, and car rental offices.
- Terminal 2 (T2): A smaller terminal exclusively for low-cost carriers such as Ryanair and easyJet. It is located a short bus ride from Terminal 1 and offers limited services compared to T1.

If you arrive at Terminal 2, you may need to transfer to Terminal 1 to access public transportation options like the metro. Shuttle buses operate regularly between the two terminals.

Airport Facilities & Services

Lisbon Airport is well-equipped to cater to travelers' needs, offering:

- Currency Exchange & ATMs: Multiple banks and exchange bureaus available.
- Wi-Fi: Free Wi-Fi throughout the airport.
- Luggage Storage: Available at Terminal 1 for short-term and long-term storage.

- Lounges: Several VIP lounges, including the ANA Lounge and TAP Premium Lounge.
- Shops & Duty-Free: A mix of international brands, Portuguese souvenirs, and tax-free shopping.
- Car Rentals: Major companies such as Hertz, Avis, Europcar, Sixt, and Enterprise have desks in Terminal 1.

2. Transportation from Lisbon Airport to the City Center

Lisbon Airport is well-connected to the city by various transport options, including metro, buses, taxis, ride-sharing, and private transfers. The journey to downtown Lisbon takes between 15 to 30 minutes, depending on the mode of transport.

1. Metro (Subway) – Fast & Affordable

The Lisbon Metro is one of the easiest and most budget-friendly ways to reach the city center from the airport.

Metro Line: Red Line (Linha Vermelha)

Station: Aeroporto (Located at Terminal 1)

Journey Time: Around 20 minutes to downtown stations like Saldanha and Baixa-Chiado

Cost: €1.80 for a single journey (€0.50 for a reusable Viva Viagem card)

Operating Hours: 6:30 AM – 1:00 AM

For visitors staying in neighborhoods such as Baixa, Chiado, or Rossio, a transfer at Alameda Station (from the Red Line to the Green Line) is required.

2. Aerobus – Convenient & Comfortable: **The Aerobus is a dedicated airport shuttle service connecting Lisbon Airport to key areas of the city.**

Routes:

Line 1: Lisbon Airport → City Center → Cais do Sodré

Line 2: Lisbon Airport → Avenida José Malhoa (Hotel District)

Journey Time: 25–35 minutes

Frequency: Every 20 minutes

Cost: €4.00 (one-way), €6.00 (round-trip)

Tickets: Can be purchased online, on the bus, or at the airport kiosks

This is a great option if you have luggage or prefer a direct connection to major hotels and tourist areas.

3. Taxis – Quick but Pricey: **Lisbon's official taxis are available outside both terminals and offer a fast way to reach your destination.**

Journey Time: 15–20 minutes to downtown Lisbon

Cost: Around €15–€20 (may vary depending on traffic and luggage fees)

Taxi Companies:

Rádio Táxis Lisboa: +351 218 119 000

Cooptáxis: +351 217 932 756

Important Tip:

Always ask for a receipt and ensure the driver uses the meter. Some drivers may try to overcharge tourists.

4. Ride-Sharing (Uber, Bolt, FreeNow): **Uber and other ride-sharing services like Bolt and FreeNow operate in Lisbon and offer a more affordable and transparent alternative to taxis.**

Cost: €8–€12 to most central areas

Pick-up Location: Rideshare pick-up zones are designated outside Terminal 1

Advantages: Fixed pricing, app-based payment, and no need for cash

5. Private Transfers – Best for Comfort & Groups: **For those seeking a hassle-free arrival experience, private transfers can be pre-booked online and provide a professional driver waiting at the airport.**

Cost: Starting at €25–€40, depending on the provider

Best For: Groups, families, business travelers, and those with extra luggage

Popular Providers:

Welcome Pickups

Suntransfers

Blacklane

6. Car Rentals – Ideal for Exploring Beyond Lisbon: **If you plan to explore beyond Lisbon (such as Sintra, Cascais, or the Algarve), renting a car can be a great option.**

Rental Companies: Hertz, Avis, Europcar, Sixt, Enterprise

Average Cost: €25–€50 per day, depending on the car model and season

Driving Tips:

Portuguese roads are well-maintained, but traffic in Lisbon can be challenging.

Parking is limited in central areas, so check if your accommodation provides parking.

With its well-organized transport system, Lisbon makes it easy for visitors to arrive and start exploring without hassle. Whether you prefer the affordability of the metro, the convenience of Aerobus, or the comfort of private transfers, the city welcomes travelers with efficiency and accessibility.

Public Transport: Metro, Trams, Buses & Ferries

Lisbon is a city that blends historic charm with modern convenience, and its public transport system plays a crucial role in connecting visitors and locals to its many neighborhoods, landmarks, and cultural hotspots. Whether you are navigating the hills of Alfama, heading to the trendy streets of Bairro Alto, or taking a scenic ride along the Tagus

River, Lisbon's public transportation network offers an affordable, efficient, and immersive way to explore the city.

From the fast and reliable Metro system to the iconic yellow trams, extensive bus routes, and scenic ferry rides, this chapter provides a detailed guide on how to get around Lisbon with ease.

1. Lisbon Metro: The Fastest Way to Travel

Overview of the Lisbon Metro System

The Lisbon Metro (Metropolitano de Lisboa) is the fastest and most efficient way to move across the city. Opened in 1959, the metro system has since expanded to include four color-coded lines, covering key districts, tourist attractions, and transportation hubs.

Lisbon Metro Lines

1. Blue Line (Linha Azul) – Reboleira ↔ Santa Apolónia

   o Connects the western and eastern parts of the city, including stops at Baixa-Chiado (historic center) and Marquês de Pombal (business district).

2. Yellow Line (Linha Amarela) – Odivelas ↔ Rato

   o Serves the northern and central parts of Lisbon, useful for reaching Entrecampos and Saldanha (business areas).

3. Green Line (Linha Verde) – Telheiras ↔ Cais do Sodré

- Runs from north to south, passing through Rossio (downtown Lisbon) and terminating at Cais do Sodré (ferry terminal and nightlife hub).
4. Red Line (Linha Vermelha) – Aeroporto ↔ São Sebastião

- The most useful line for airport transfers, connecting Lisbon Portela Airport (Aeroporto station) to the city center in about 20 minutes.

Using the Metro: Tickets & Prices

- Single journey ticket: €1.80
- 24-hour unlimited pass (valid on metro, trams, buses, and some ferries): €6.80
- Viva Viagem Card: A rechargeable travel card (€0.50) used for metro, buses, and trams.

The metro runs daily from 6:30 AM to 1:00 AM, making it a convenient option for both early risers and night owls.

When to Use the Metro

- Best for: Quick travel across Lisbon, airport transfers, and reaching major hubs.
- Avoid during: Rush hours (8:00-9:30 AM and 6:00-7:30 PM) when it gets crowded.

2. Lisbon's Iconic Trams: A Ride Through History

A Glimpse into Lisbon's Tram Network

Lisbon's trams (Elétricos) are an iconic part of the city's transportation system, offering both practical transportation and a nostalgic journey through its historic streets. The network includes both modern and vintage trams, with the most famous being the classic yellow Remodelado trams that date back to the 1930s.

Must-Ride Trams in Lisbon

1. Tram 28 (Eléctrico 28) – The Most Famous Route

   o Route: Martim Moniz ↔ Campo de Ourique (Prazeres)
   o Why ride? Travels through Lisbon's most scenic neighborhoods, including Alfama, Graça, Baixa, and Estrela.
   o Best time to ride: Early morning (before 9:00 AM) or late evening (after 8:00 PM) to avoid crowds.

2. Tram 12 (Eléctrico 12) – A Shorter Alternative to Tram 28

   o Route: A circular loop through Baixa and Alfama.
   o Why ride? A great option if Tram 28 is too crowded.

3. Tram 15 (Eléctrico 15E) – The Route to Belém

   o Route: Cais do Sodré ↔ Belém
   o Why ride? The fastest way to reach Belém Tower, Jerónimos Monastery, and Pastéis de Belém.
   o Alternative: If the tram is too packed, take bus 728 to Belém.

Taxis, Ride-Sharing & Car Rentals

Lisbon is a city of steep hills, historic streets, and scenic waterfronts, making transportation an important factor in any visitor's experience. While public transport, including trams and buses, is extensive, taxis, ride-sharing services, and car rentals offer convenience, flexibility, and speed, depending on your needs.

Whether you are heading to your hotel from the airport, exploring different neighborhoods, or planning a day trip outside the city, understanding how to use these transportation options effectively can save time and money. This chapter provides a comprehensive guide on taxis, ride-sharing apps, and car rentals in Lisbon, along with practical tips for navigating the city efficiently.

Taxis in Lisbon: What You Need to Know

Taxis in Lisbon are widely available and are an efficient way to get around, particularly for short distances, when carrying luggage, or when public transport is less convenient.

1. How to Identify a Taxi in Lisbon

Most taxis in Lisbon are beige with a green and black taxi sign on the roof. Older models may still be black with a green roof, though this color scheme is becoming less common. Official taxis always have a meter and a driver identification badge displayed inside the vehicle.

2. Taxi Fares & Pricing

Taxis in Lisbon operate on a metered system, ensuring transparent pricing. Below is a breakdown of the typical fares:

Type of Fare	Estimated Price
Base fare (daytime)	€3.50
Base fare (nighttime, weekends, and holidays)	€4.00
Per kilometer	€0.47

Waiting time per hour	€14.80
Airport surcharge	€1.60
Luggage fee (for items over 55x35x20cm)	€1.60 per item

For short rides within the city center, expect to pay between €6 and €10. A taxi from Lisbon Airport to downtown areas such as Baixa or Chiado typically costs between €12 and €20, depending on traffic and time of day.

3. How to Get a Taxi in Lisbon

There are several ways to find a taxi in Lisbon:

Hailing one on the street – Taxis are common in tourist areas, main squares, and transportation hubs.

Taxi stands (Praças de Táxis) – Designated taxi ranks are located in key areas such as:

Lisbon Airport

Rossio Square

Cais do Sodré

Avenida da Liberdade

Calling a taxi service or using a taxi-hailing app – Some reputable taxi companies include:

Radio Taxis: +351 218 119 000

CoopTaxis: +351 217 932 756

AutoTaxis: +351 218 111 100

For a more convenient experience, apps like Bolt and FREE NOW allow travelers to book a licensed taxi using their smartphones.

4. Pros & Cons of Using Taxis in Lisbon

Pros:

Readily available throughout the city.

More affordable than taxis in other European capitals.

Useful for airport transfers and when carrying luggage.

Cons:

Some drivers may attempt to overcharge tourists, particularly from the airport.

- Not all taxis accept card payments, so carrying cash is advisable.
- Limited English proficiency among some drivers.

Ride-Sharing Services in Lisbon

For travelers who prefer digital payments and pre-set fares, ride-sharing services offer a more convenient alternative to taxis. These services are often more affordable, with the added benefit of real-time tracking and easier communication.

1. Popular Ride-Sharing Apps in Lisbon

- Uber – The most widely used ride-sharing service in Lisbon, offering:
  o UberX (budget option)
  o Uber Black (premium vehicles)

o   Uber Green (electric vehicles)
- Bolt – Usually cheaper than Uber, with quick availability and reliable service.
- FREE NOW – Allows users to book licensed taxis as well as ride-sharing vehicles.

2. Advantages of Ride-Sharing Over Taxis

- Fixed fares – Eliminates concerns about overcharging.
- Cashless transactions – Secure and hassle-free payments through the app.
- Real-time tracking – Passengers can track their driver's location.
- Vehicle options – Users can select different ride types based on budget and comfort preferences.

3. Estimated Costs for Ride-Sharing Services

Route	UberX Fare (Estimated)	Bolt Fare (Estimated)
Lisbon Airport → City Center	€8 - €12	€7 - €10
Baixa → Belém	€6 - €9	€5 - €8
Alfama → Bairro Alto	€4 - €7	€3 - €6

Ride-sharing is highly recommended for travelers who want to avoid negotiating fares or prefer digital payment methods.

Car Rentals in Lisbon

Renting a car in Lisbon can be a great option for travelers planning to explore beyond the city. However, for navigating central Lisbon, a car is often unnecessary due to traffic congestion, limited parking, and an efficient public transport system.

1. When to Consider Renting a Car

If planning day trips to Sintra, Cascais, Évora, or the Algarve.

If traveling with family or a group, making shared costs lower.

If preferring the freedom and flexibility of driving through Portugal's countryside.

2. Where to Rent a Car in Lisbon

The best locations for car rentals include:

Lisbon Airport (Humberto Delgado Airport) – Most international rental companies operate here.

Downtown Lisbon – Avenida da Liberdade has several rental agencies.

Top car rental companies in Lisbon include:

Hertz

Europcar

Sixt

Enterprise

3. Driving & Parking Rules in Lisbon

In Portugal, driving is on the right side of the road.

The legal driving age is 18, but most rental companies require drivers to be at least 21.

Tolls are common on Portuguese highways, so check if your rental car includes an electronic toll device.

Parking in central Lisbon is limited and often expensive. Using paid parking garages is recommended.

4. Estimated Car Rental Costs

Car Type	Daily Rental Price
Economy Car	€20 - €40
Mid-Size Car	€40 - €60
SUV	€60 - €100

Gasoline prices in Portugal range from €1.80 to €2.00 per liter, making fuel costs an important consideration.

5. Pros & Cons of Renting a Car in Lisbon

Pros:

Ideal for day trips and road trips outside Lisbon.

Provides flexibility and independence.

Cons:

Traffic congestion in central Lisbon can be frustrating.

- Expensive toll roads when traveling long distances.
- Limited and costly parking in tourist areas.

Walking & Biking in the City

Lisbon is a city best explored on foot, with its winding streets, hidden alleyways, and stunning viewpoints making every walk an adventure. However, the city's hilly terrain, cobblestone sidewalks, and sometimes unpredictable weather require visitors to be well-prepared for a mix of charming strolls and challenging climbs.

For those who prefer a two-wheeled approach, Lisbon's biking infrastructure has been improving in recent years, with new cycling lanes, bike-sharing services, and scenic riverside routes making it increasingly bike-friendly. This chapter provides a detailed guide on how to explore Lisbon by walking and cycling, covering the best pedestrian routes, cycling paths, tips for navigating the city's topography, and essential information on renting bikes.

Walking in Lisbon: A City Meant for Exploration

Lisbon is one of the most walkable capitals in Europe, but it also comes with a few challenges. The city's seven hills, historic but uneven cobblestone pavements, and narrow alleyways can make walking both delightful and demanding. However, the effort is often rewarded with breathtaking viewpoints, charming street scenes, and unexpected discoveries.

1. Best Neighborhoods for Walking

Certain districts in Lisbon are perfect for exploring on foot, offering a combination of history, culture, and scenic beauty.

- Baixa and Chiado
  The heart of downtown Lisbon, Baixa is a flat and highly walkable area filled with neoclassical buildings, large squares, and grand boulevards. Rua Augusta, the main pedestrian street, connects Praça do Comércio to Rossio Square, offering lively cafés, street performers, and excellent shopping. Chiado, just next to Baixa, is an elegant neighborhood filled with bookstores, historic cafés, and cultural landmarks.

- Alfama
  One of the most picturesque yet challenging areas to walk in, Alfama is Lisbon's oldest district, characterized by steep, narrow streets and hidden courtyards. The climb to São Jorge Castle is rewarded with spectacular city views, while wandering through the maze of alleyways reveals traditional Fado houses, colorful azulejo facades, and local markets.

- Bairro Alto and Principe Real
  Bairro Alto, known for its nightlife and bohemian atmosphere, is best explored on foot during the day when it is quieter and allows visitors to admire the street art, boutique shops, and tiled buildings. Principe Real, just above Bairro Alto, offers green parks, concept stores, and great cafés, making it a pleasant area for a relaxed stroll.

- Belém
  Unlike the central neighborhoods, Belém is flat and open, making it an ideal place for a leisurely walk along the Tagus River. The district is home to Jerónimos Monastery, Belém Tower, and the

Monument to the Discoveries, all of which can be visited on foot while enjoying the scenic waterfront.

2. Best Walking Routes in Lisbon

Lisbon's hilly terrain may discourage some travelers, but several routes are designed for both casual walkers and serious explorers.

- Historic Lisbon Walk (3-4 hours)

  o Start at Praça do Comércio, one of Lisbon's grandest squares.
  o Walk up Rua Augusta towards Rossio Square.
  o Explore Chiado, stopping at Café A Brasileira for a coffee.
  o Climb to Carmo Convent and enjoy the historic ruins.
  o Continue to Miradouro de São Pedro de Alcântara for panoramic views.

- Alfama & São Jorge Castle Walk (2-3 hours)

  o Begin at Sé de Lisboa (Lisbon Cathedral).
  o Wander through the narrow streets of Alfama, passing Fado houses.
  o Climb to São Jorge Castle and explore the fortress.
  o Descend towards Miradouro de Santa Luzia, a viewpoint overlooking the rooftops and river.

- Belém Riverside Walk (2-3 hours, flat terrain)

  o Start at Jerónimos Monastery and admire the intricate Manueline architecture.
  o Walk to Pastéis de Belém for the city's most famous custard tarts.
  o Stroll along the Tagus River towards Belém Tower.

    o   Visit the Monument to the Discoveries and the MAAT Museum.

3. Tips for Walking in Lisbon

- Wear Comfortable Shoes Lisbon's sidewalks are made of small, slippery cobblestones, known as calçada portuguesa. Flat, rubber-soled shoes are recommended, especially if walking in hilly areas.

- Use Public Transport to Avoid Tough Climbs
  If a route is too steep, take a tram, funicular, or elevator to save energy. The Santa Justa Lift, Ascensor da Glória, and Tram 28 all help navigate the city's inclines.

- Stay Hydrated
  Lisbon's warm climate can be exhausting, particularly in summer. Many public fountains provide drinkable water, so carrying a refillable bottle is advisable.

- Be Mindful of Pickpockets
  Popular tourist areas, such as Baixa and tram stops, can attract pickpockets. Keep belongings secure, especially in crowded spaces.

Biking in Lisbon: A Growing Trend

Cycling in Lisbon has become more popular in recent years, thanks to improved bike lanes and an increasing number of rental options. While some areas are steep and challenging, the riverfront and certain flat districts are ideal for biking.

1. Best Cycling Routes in Lisbon

- Tagus River Path (Cais do Sodré to Belém)

- o A flat, scenic route along the river, perfect for casual cyclists.
- o Pass by LX Factory, Belém Tower, and the Monument to the Discoveries.
- o Ideal for a relaxed ride with waterfront views.
- Parque das Nações Cycle Path
  - o A modern, bike-friendly area with wide lanes and contemporary architecture.
  - o Start at Oriente Station and ride along the waterfront.
  - o Visit the Lisbon Oceanarium and Vasco da Gama Bridge.
- Monsanto Forest Park Route
  - o A nature-filled ride in Lisbon's largest green space.
  - o Perfect for mountain biking and trail cycling.
  - o Offers fresh air and escape from the urban landscape.

2. Bike Rentals and Bike-Sharing in Lisbon

Several companies offer bike rentals, with options ranging from standard bicycles to electric bikes (which are recommended for Lisbon's hills).

- Gira – Lisbon's Bike-Sharing Service
  - o Lisbon's official bike-sharing program, available at docking stations across the city.
  - o Offers electric and traditional bikes at affordable rates.
  - o App-based system, requiring a quick registration process.
- Bike Rentals & Tours

o Bike Iberia (Located in Baixa, offers city and e-bike rentals).
o Lisbon Bike Rentals (Mountain and road bikes, guided tours available).

3. Tips for Cycling in Lisbon

- Use an Electric Bike for Steep Areas
  While flat districts like Belém and Parque das Nações are easy to bike through, steeper areas like Alfama and Bairro Alto can be difficult. An e-bike is a great alternative.

- Be Cautious in Traffic
  Lisbon's roads can be narrow and busy, especially in historic areas. Stick to designated bike lanes where available.

- Lock Your Bike
  Always secure rented bikes, as theft can be a concern in tourist areas.

Chapter 3

Best Neighborhoods to Stay In Lisbon

Lisbon is a city of contrasts, where history meets modernity, tradition blends with innovation, and each neighborhood offers a unique atmosphere and experience. Choosing the right place to stay can shape your trip, influencing how you experience the city, how easily you can access major attractions, and even how you spend your evenings.

This chapter explores four of Lisbon's most popular neighborhoods—Baixa & Chiado, Alfama, Bairro Alto, and Belém—highlighting what makes each area unique, the types of accommodations available, and the pros and cons of staying in each location.

Each of Lisbon's neighborhoods has a distinct personality, from the central and lively streets of Baixa and Chiado, to the historic charm of Alfama, the vibrant nightlife of Bairro Alto, and the riverside tranquility of Belém. Choosing the right district depends on your interests, budget, and the type of experience you want in Portugal's capital.

Baixa & Chiado: Central & Lively

Baixa and Chiado are the heart of Lisbon, offering the perfect mix of convenience, accessibility, and cultural attractions. This area is ideal for first-time visitors who want to stay in the center of the action, surrounded by historic squares, grand architecture, shopping streets, and some of the city's most famous landmarks.

Why Stay in Baixa & Chiado?

- Central location: Walking distance to major attractions like Praça do Comércio, Elevador de Santa Justa, and Rossio Square.
- Great public transport connections: Close to metro stations, trams, and train lines to Sintra and Cascais.
- Excellent dining and shopping: A mix of traditional Portuguese restaurants, modern cafés, and high-end shops.

Top Attractions in the Area

- Rua Augusta: The city's most famous pedestrian street, lined with shops and cafés.
- Santa Justa Lift: An iconic iron elevator offering stunning views of the city.
- Praça do Comércio: A grand waterfront square, perfect for people-watching.
- Carmo Convent: A historic church ruin that tells the story of Lisbon's 1755 earthquake.

Types of Accommodation

- Luxury Hotels: The Baixa and Chiado districts are home to some of Lisbon's finest hotels, including Pousada de Lisboa and Bairro Alto Hotel.
- Boutique Hotels: Stylish and unique options like Lisboa Carmo Hotel and The Lumiares Hotel & Spa.
- Budget Stays: Mid-range and budget hotels such as Hotel Mundial offer affordability without sacrificing location.

Pros & Cons of Staying in Baixa & Chiado

Pros	Cons
Very central, making it easy to explore the city on foot	Can be crowded, especially during peak tourist season

Great for first-time visitors due to accessibility	Hotels tend to be more expensive
Well-connected to public transportation	The area can be noisy, especially around major streets

Alfama: Historic & Charming: Alfama is **Lisbon's oldest district, filled with narrow streets, traditional Fado music, and medieval charm.** Staying in Alfama feels like stepping back in time, surrounded by **ancient buildings, hidden courtyards, and spectacular viewpoints.**

Why Stay in Alfama?

Rich history: The area retains much of Lisbon's medieval layout, making it perfect for history lovers.

Authentic atmosphere: Traditional Portuguese culture is alive here, from small family-owned restaurants to Fado music echoing in the alleyways.

Breathtaking views: Many accommodations offer views over the Tagus River and Lisbon's famous red rooftops.

Top Attractions in the Area

São Jorge Castle: A historic fortress with some of the best panoramic views of the city.

Sé de Lisboa (Lisbon Cathedral): One of the most iconic religious landmarks in Lisbon.

Miradouros (Viewpoints): Miradouro de Santa Luzia and Miradouro das Portas do Sol provide stunning scenic spots.

Fado Houses: Traditional restaurants where you can experience Lisbon's soul-stirring Fado music.

Pros & Cons of Staying in Alfama

Pros	Cons
Unique, historic charm	Streets are steep and difficult to navigate with luggage
Great for an immersive local experience	Public transport access is limited
Stunning views from many accommodations	Can be quiet at night with fewer nightlife options

Bairro Alto: Nightlife & Bohemian Vibes: Bairro Alto is **Lisbon's nightlife hub, where narrow streets come alive after sunset with bars, live music, and late-night revelers.** During the day, it is a peaceful neighborhood with **independent shops, artistic cafés, and colorful street art.**

Why Stay in Bairro Alto?

Ideal for nightlife lovers: The area is famous for its vibrant bar scene and buzzing atmosphere.

Cultural hotspots: Home to Fado houses, street art, and experimental restaurants.

Great mix of budget and boutique accommodations: From affordable hostels to stylish boutique hotels.

Top Attractions in the Area

Miradouro de São Pedro de Alcântara: One of Lisbon's best viewpoints, offering panoramic city views.

Pink Street (Rua Nova do Carvalho): A trendy nightlife spot with bars and clubs.

Elevador da Glória: A funicular connecting Bairro Alto to the lower part of the city.

Pros & Cons of Staying in Bairro Alto

Pros	Cons
Best nightlife in the city	Can be noisy at night, especially on weekends
Bohemian and artistic vibe	Not ideal for light sleepers
Many budget-friendly accommodations	Hilly streets require some effort to navigate

Belém: Riverside & Cultural

Belém is known for its grand monuments, scenic riverfront, and relaxed atmosphere. Unlike the central areas, Belém offers more open spaces and a slower pace, making it ideal for travelers who want a peaceful stay near historical landmarks.

Why Stay in Belém?

Cultural significance: Home to Lisbon's most famous landmarks, including Belém Tower and Jerónimos Monastery.

Scenic riverside setting: Perfect for relaxing walks along the Tagus River.

Less tourist congestion: While busy during the day, Belém is quieter at night compared to central Lisbon.

Pros & Cons of Staying in Belém

Pros	Cons

Beautiful, relaxing riverside environment	Far from Lisbon's nightlife and city center
Rich in history and culture	Fewer accommodation options
Great for a slower-paced stay	Requires public transport for exploring central Lisbon

Top Hotels, Hostels & Airbnb Recommendations

Lisbon is a city that caters to every type of traveler, offering a diverse range of accommodations from luxurious five-star hotels to budget-friendly hostels and unique Airbnb stays. Whether visitors seek a historic boutique hotel, a lively backpacker's hostel, or a private apartment with a view of the Tagus River, Lisbon has no shortage of options.

This chapter provides a comprehensive guide to the best places to stay, categorized by accommodation type and budget. It also includes recommendations for different traveler preferences, from romantic getaways to family-friendly stays and solo traveler hubs.

Top Hotels in Lisbon

Lisbon's hotel scene is vibrant, with a mix of historic charm and modern luxury. The best hotels in the city are often located in Baixa, Chiado, Avenida da Liberdade, and Belém, offering easy access to attractions, restaurants, and public transport.

1. Luxury Hotels (5-Star and High-End Stays)

For travelers looking for world-class service, elegant decor, and top-tier amenities, Lisbon's luxury hotels provide an unforgettable experience.

- Olissippo Lapa Palace

  o A stunning 19th-century palace-turned-hotel in a quiet residential area.
  o Features an outdoor pool, lush gardens, and river views.
  o Ideal for romantic getaways and luxury travelers.

  Address: Rua do Pau de Bandeira 4, 1249-021 Lisboa, Portugal
  Phone: +351 21 394 9494

- Four Seasons Hotel Ritz Lisbon

  o A classic five-star hotel with exceptional service and luxurious interiors.
  o Offers panoramic views of the city, a rooftop running track, and a top-tier spa.
  o Located near Avenida da Liberdade, Lisbon's luxury shopping district.

  Address: R. Rodrigo da Fonseca 88, 1099-039 Lisboa, Portugal
  Phone: +351 21 381 1400

- Pestana Palace Lisboa

  o A historic palace-turned-hotel listed as a national monument.
  o Features lavish interiors, beautiful gardens, and a Michelin-starred restaurant.
  o Perfect for those who appreciate historic elegance.

Address: R. Jau 54, 1300-314 Lisboa, Portugal
Phone: +351 21 361 5600

2. Mid-Range Hotels (3- and 4-Star Comfort)

For travelers seeking comfort, convenience, and affordability, Lisbon offers a great selection of mid-range hotels with excellent service and stylish decor.

- Hotel da Baixa

  o A charming boutique hotel in the heart of downtown Lisbon.
  o Features modern rooms with traditional Portuguese design elements.
  o Located close to Praça do Comércio, the Santa Justa Lift, and Alfama.

  Address: Rua da Prata 231, 1100-417 Lisboa, Portugal
  Phone: +351 21 012 7450

- Memmo Alfama Hotel

  o A stylish design hotel with a rooftop terrace and breathtaking city views.
  o Located in the historic Alfama district, ideal for culture lovers and photographers.
  o Offers wine tastings and a small infinity pool overlooking Lisbon's rooftops.

  Address: Tv. Merceeiras 27, 1100-348 Lisboa, Portugal
  Phone: +351 21 049 5660

- Lisboa Carmo Hotel

- Located in the trendy Chiado district, surrounded by restaurants and cafés.
- Offers modern rooms with a touch of traditional Portuguese decor.
- A great option for those wanting to stay in a lively but elegant area.

Address: R. da Oliveira ao Carmo 1A, 1200-307 Lisboa, Portugal
Phone: +351 21 326 4710

3. Budget-Friendly Hotels (Affordable & Comfortable)

For travelers on a budget who still want a comfortable stay with good amenities, these hotels provide great value for money.

- My Story Hotel Rossio

  - A well-rated affordable hotel in the heart of Lisbon.
  - Located in Rossio Square, within walking distance of top attractions.
  - Great for budget-conscious travelers who want a central location.

  Address: Praça Dom Pedro IV 59, 1100-200 Lisboa, Portugal
  Phone: +351 21 340 0380

- Moxy Lisbon City

  - A modern and stylish budget hotel with trendy interiors.

- o Offers affordable rates, a rooftop pool, and a lively atmosphere.
- o Ideal for young travelers and digital nomads.

Address: Av. Duque de Loulé 2 a 8, 1050-090 Lisboa, Portugal
Phone: +351 21 020 2929

- Hotel LX Rossio

  - o Located in the Baixa district, offering simple yet clean rooms.
  - o An excellent budget-friendly option with easy access to public transport.

Address: R. da Assunção 52, 1100-044 Lisboa, Portugal
Phone: +351 21 342 7625

Best Hostels in Lisbon

Lisbon has one of the best hostel scenes in Europe, with beautifully designed spaces, social atmospheres, and great amenities. Hostels in Lisbon cater to solo travelers, backpackers, and budget-conscious visitors, offering both dormitory and private room options.

1. Best Social Hostels (Great for Meeting People)

- Yes! Lisbon Hostel

  - o A highly rated social hostel with daily group dinners and pub crawls.
  - o Offers clean dorms and private rooms, friendly staff, and great activities.

- o Ideal for solo travelers and those looking to make new friends.

  Address: R. de São Julião 148, 1100-527 Lisboa, Portugal

  Phone: +351 21 342 7171

- Home Lisbon Hostel

  - o Known for its legendary family dinners hosted by "Mama", the owner's mother.
  - o A warm and friendly atmosphere with spacious dorms and a cozy common area.
  - o Great for travelers looking for a home-like stay with a social vibe.

  Address: R. de São Nicolau 13 2Esq, 1100-547 Lisboa, Portugal

  Phone: +351 21 888 5312

2. Best Boutique & Design Hostels

- The Independente Hostel & Suites

  - o A boutique-style hostel with artistic decor and a hip atmosphere.
  - o Located in Bairro Alto, surrounded by Lisbon's best nightlife.
  - o Offers both dormitories and stylish private suites.

  Address: R. de São Pedro de Alcântara 83, 1250-238 Lisboa, Portugal

  Phone: +351 21 346 1381

- Lisbon Destination Hostel

  - o Housed in the historic Rossio Train Station, blending old-world charm with modern comfort.

o Offers a beautiful common area, stylish dorms, and an excellent location.

Address: Estação do Rossio, Largo do Duque de Cadaval 2º andar, 1200-160 Lisboa, Portugal
Phone: +351 21 346 6457

3. Best Budget Hostels

- We Love F. Tourists Hostel

  o A small and friendly hostel offering budget stays in a central location.
  o Provides free walking tours, a cozy lounge, and a relaxed atmosphere.

  Address: R. dos Fanqueiros 267, 1100-230 Lisboa, Portugal
  Phone: +351 21 887 1327
- Sunset Destination Hostel

  o Features a rooftop terrace, pool, and a relaxed social setting.
  o Located near Cais do Sodré station, perfect for exploring Lisbon's nightlife.

  Address: PC Duque da Terceira, 1200-161 Lisboa, Portugal
  Phone: +351 913 391 800

Best Airbnb & Vacation Rentals in Lisbon: For travelers who prefer **private accommodations with a local feel**, Lisbon offers a wide selection of **Airbnb rentals and vacation apartments**.

1. Best Airbnbs for Couples & Romantic Stays

- Riverside Loft in Alfama

    o A cozy apartment with stunning views over the Tagus River.
    o Features traditional Portuguese tiles and a private balcony.

  Address: Rua dos Bacalhoeiros 12, Lisbon 1100-070 Portugal
  Phone: +351 218 860 129

- Chiado Penthouse with Terrace

    o A modern, stylish apartment with a spacious outdoor terrace.
    o Perfect for romantic dinners with a view of the city skyline.

  Address: Largo do Chiado 5, Santa Maria Maior, 1200-108 Lisboa, Portugal

2. Best Family-Friendly Airbnbs

- Spacious Apartment in Principe Real

    o A large and well-equipped apartment in a quiet but central neighborhood.
    o Offers multiple bedrooms, a fully stocked kitchen, and family-friendly amenities.
- Belém Riverfront Apartment

- Located near Belém's attractions, offering easy access to family-friendly sites.
- Spacious and comfortable for families with children.

3. Best Airbnbs for Digital Nomads & Long Stays

- Modern Apartment in Marvila (Lisbon's Creative Hub)
  - A stylish and spacious apartment with a dedicated workspace.
  - Located in an up-and-coming neighborhood with coworking spaces and cafés.
- Lisbon Loft with Fast Wi-Fi in Santos
  - A bright and minimalist loft with a strong internet connection.
  - Near trendy cafés, art galleries, and coworking spaces.

No matter the budget or travel style, Lisbon offers accommodation options for everyone. Whether in a luxurious palace, a stylish boutique hotel, a lively hostel, or a charming Airbnb, every stay in Lisbon promises comfort and charm.

Chapter 4

Belém Tower & Jerónimos Monastery

Lisbon is a city filled with history, charm, and remarkable landmarks, but few places capture the essence of Portugal's rich past as well as Belém Tower (Torre de Belém) and Jerónimos Monastery (Mosteiro dos Jerónimos). These two UNESCO World Heritage Sites are among the most iconic attractions in Lisbon, deeply intertwined with the Age of Exploration and Portugal's maritime legacy. Located in the picturesque riverside district of Belém, they stand as symbols of Portugal's golden age of discovery, attracting visitors with their architectural beauty, historical significance, and cultural impact.

This chapter explores the history, architecture, and visitor experience of these must-see landmarks, as well as practical tips for making the most of a visit.

Belém Tower: The Guardian of Lisbon's Shores
A Brief History of Belém Tower

Belém Tower, built between 1514 and 1520, is one of Lisbon's most famous landmarks and a key symbol of Portugal's maritime power during the Age of Exploration. Originally constructed as a fortress to guard the entrance to the Tagus River, it played a crucial role in defending Lisbon from potential invaders.

Commissioned by King Manuel I, the tower was designed by the architect Francisco de Arruda and is a striking example of Manueline architecture, a Portuguese style that blends Gothic, Moorish, and Renaissance influences. Over the centuries, Belém Tower has served multiple functions, including as a prison, customs checkpoint, and lighthouse.

In 1983, it was designated a UNESCO World Heritage Site along with Jerónimos Monastery due to its historical and architectural significance.

Architectural Features of Belém Tower

Belém Tower is one of the finest surviving examples of Manueline architecture, distinguished by its intricate stone carvings, maritime motifs, and Moorish-inspired design elements.

- The Bastion: The lower portion of the tower, shaped like a ship's bow, was designed to house cannons and artillery for coastal defense. Today, visitors can walk along the bastion and enjoy panoramic views of the Tagus River.
- The Four Turrets: At each corner of the tower, small Moorish-style turrets with decorative stonework add to the fortress's unique charm.
- Renaissance Loggia: The elegant balconies and windows, adorned with ornate stone carvings, showcase the influence of the Renaissance period.
- The Statue of Our Lady of Safe Homecoming: A tribute to Portugal's explorers, this statue was meant to protect sailors as they embarked on long sea voyages.

Visiting Belém Tower: What to Expect

Belém Tower is one of the most visited sites in Lisbon, and exploring it offers a fascinating glimpse into Portugal's naval history.

- Inside the Tower: Visitors can climb the narrow spiral staircase to the top, where they will be rewarded with spectacular views of the river, 25 de Abril Bridge, and the surrounding Belém district.
- Underground Dungeons: The lower levels once served as prison cells, where captives were held before being transported to distant colonies.
- Best Time to Visit: Early mornings or late afternoons are ideal to avoid crowds, as queues can be long during peak hours.

Tips for Visiting Belém Tower

- Opening Hours: Typically open from 10:00 AM to 6:30 PM (summer) and 10:00 AM to 5:30 PM (winter). Closed on Mondays.

- Entry Fees: Tickets cost around €8, but combination tickets with Jerónimos Monastery offer a better deal.
- Getting There: Take the train 15E from downtown Lisbon, which stops right near the tower.

Jerónimos Monastery: A Masterpiece of Manueline Architecture

The History of Jerónimos Monastery: Jerónimos Monastery, a grand **monument to Portugal's Age of Discovery**, was built in **1501** to commemorate **Vasco da Gama's successful voyage to India**. The monastery was commissioned by **King Manuel I**, who funded the construction with **wealth from the spice trade**. It was originally home to the

Order of Saint Jerome (Hieronymite monks), who provided spiritual guidance to sailors and prayed for their safe journeys.

The monastery was designed by the architect Diogo de Boitaca, who introduced the intricate Manueline style, later continued by other architects such as João de Castilho. Its construction took almost 100 years to complete, and today it stands as one of the most impressive architectural achievements in Europe.

Architectural Highlights of Jerónimos Monastery: Jerónimos Monastery is an **architectural masterpiece**, featuring intricate carvings, grand cloisters, and impressive religious symbolism.

- The South Portal: This magnificent entrance, designed by João de Castilho, is adorned with elaborate stonework, including statues of Saint Jerome, King Manuel I, and various religious figures.
- The Cloisters: Considered one of the most beautiful in the world, the two-story cloisters feature delicate stone tracery, maritime motifs, and peaceful courtyards.
- The Church of Santa Maria de Belém: This grand church features a stunning ribbed vault ceiling, massive columns, and the tombs of Portugal's most legendary figures.
- Tombs of Vasco da Gama & Luís de Camões: Inside the church, visitors can pay their respects to Vasco da Gama, the famed navigator, and Luís de Camões, Portugal's national poet.

Visiting Jerónimos Monastery: (What to Expect): Walking through Jerónimos Monastery is like stepping back into Portugal's golden age. Highlights of a visit include:

- Exploring the Grand Cloisters: The peaceful cloisters are perfect for taking in the intricate Manueline details and stunning arches.
- Admiring the Ornate Church Interior: The church's vast nave and delicate stone carvings make it a truly awe-inspiring space.
- Learning About Portugal's Maritime History: The monastery's connection to Vasco da Gama and the Age of Exploration adds historical depth to the visit.

Tips for Visiting Jerónimos Monastery

- Opening Hours: Open from 10:00 AM to 6:30 PM (summer) and 10:00 AM to 5:30 PM (winter). Closed on Mondays.
- Entry Fees: Around €10, with discounts for students and seniors. Combination tickets with Belém Tower are available.
- Getting There: The monastery is a short walk from Belém Tower, and can be reached by tram 15E.

Belém: More to Explore

While Belém Tower and Jerónimos Monastery are the main highlights, the Belém district has much more to offer:

- Pastéis de Belém: No visit to Belém is complete without tasting a warm, flaky Pastel de Nata from the legendary bakery that originated the famous Portuguese custard tart.
- Monument to the Discoveries: A striking riverside monument dedicated to Portugal's greatest explorers, featuring a 52-meter-high sculpture of Prince Henry the Navigator.
- Belém Cultural Center: A modern museum space housing art exhibitions and cultural performances.

- National Coach Museum: Showcasing a remarkable collection of ornate royal carriages from different centuries.

São Jorge Castle & Alfama's Miradouros

Lisbon is a city of stunning views, rich history, and charming streets, and no place captures its

essence better than São Jorge Castle and the miradouros (viewpoints) of Alfama. Perched on one of the city's highest hills, São Jorge Castle offers an incredible journey through Lisbon's Moorish and medieval past, while Alfama's viewpoints provide breathtaking panoramic scenes of the city and the Tagus River.

These two attractions are essential stops for any traveler, whether you are drawn to historical sites, photography, or simply experiencing Lisbon's unique charm. This chapter takes you through the history, highlights, and tips for exploring São Jorge Castle and Alfama's best viewpoints.

São Jorge Castle: A Journey Through Lisbon's History

A Fortress Overlooking the City

São Jorge Castle (Castelo de São Jorge) is one of Lisbon's most recognizable landmarks. Located in the historic Alfama district, it dominates the skyline with its ancient walls and towers. Originally built by the Moors in the 11th century, the castle has witnessed centuries of battles, sieges, and royal history.

This fortress served as a military stronghold during the Moorish occupation before being recaptured by Christian forces in 1147, led by King Afonso I (Afonso Henriques). It later became a royal palace and continued to be an important part of Portuguese history. Today, it is one of the most visited sites in Lisbon, offering stunning views, archaeological discoveries, and an immersive experience into Lisbon's past.

Exploring the Castle: What to See

1. The Castle Walls & Towers

One of the highlights of São Jorge Castle is the imposing stone walls and towers, which visitors can climb to admire

360-degree views of Lisbon. The most famous towers include:

- Torre de Menagem: The central keep, offering spectacular views over the city.
- Torre do Tombo: Historically used as a royal archive.
- Torre de São Lourenço: One of the best spots for sunset photography.

As you walk along the castle's battlements, you'll see Alfama's red rooftops, the Tagus River, and landmarks like the 25 de Abril Bridge and Praça do Comércio.

2. The Archaeological Site

São Jorge Castle is not just a medieval fortress—it is also an archaeological treasure. Excavations have uncovered ruins dating back to the Iron Age, the Moorish period, and the 15th century. Visitors can explore these remains and learn about the various civilizations that have influenced Lisbon.

3. The Camera Obscura

A unique attraction within the castle is the Camera Obscura, a periscope-like device that offers a live, real-time view of the city. Located in one of the castle's towers, this optical system provides a detailed look at Lisbon from a fascinating perspective.

4. The Castle Gardens & Peacocks

São Jorge Castle is home to beautiful gardens with native plants and trees, where visitors can relax while taking in the stunning views. The area is also famous for its resident peacocks, which roam freely and add to the castle's magical atmosphere.

How to Visit São Jorge Castle

- Opening Hours: Open daily from 9:00 AM to 9:00 PM (summer) and 9:00 AM to 6:00 PM (winter).
- Ticket Prices: General admission is around €10, with discounts for students and seniors.
- How to Get There: Take the famous Tram 28, walk through the charming streets of Alfama, or take a taxi/Uber.
- Best Time to Visit: Arrive early in the morning to avoid crowds or visit just before sunset for the best views.

Alfama's Miradouros: The Best Viewpoints in Lisbon

After exploring São Jorge Castle, take some time to wander through Alfama, Lisbon's oldest and most picturesque neighborhood. Known for its narrow cobblestone streets, traditional houses, and hidden courtyards, Alfama is also home to some of Lisbon's most spectacular miradouros (viewpoints).

These viewpoints offer breathtaking views of the city and river, making them perfect spots for photos, relaxation, and appreciating Lisbon's beauty.

Top Miradouros in Alfama

1. Miradouro de Santa Luzia

One of the most romantic and picturesque viewpoints in Lisbon, Miradouro de Santa Luzia is famous for its azulejo-covered walls (traditional Portuguese tiles), bougainvillea-covered pergolas, and stunning views over Alfama's rooftops and the Tagus River.

- What to Expect:

  o Beautiful blue-and-white tile panels depicting Lisbon's history.
  o A relaxing terrace with benches and shaded areas.
  o A great place to watch the sunrise or sunset.

- Nearby Attractions:

  o Igreja de Santa Luzia (small church with a beautiful facade).
  o Tram 28 stop, making it easy to access from other parts of the city.

2. Miradouro das Portas do Sol

A short walk from Miradouro de Santa Luzia, this viewpoint offers one of the best panoramic views of Lisbon. From here, you can see:

- The red rooftops of Alfama.
- The Tagus River and cruise ships docked at the port.
- The dome of the National Pantheon and São Vicente de Fora Monastery.

This viewpoint is also home to a bronze statue of Saint Vincent, the patron saint of Lisbon, holding a boat and two ravens, which symbolize the city's history.

- Best Time to Visit: Late afternoon for the golden hour effect over the rooftops.
- Nearby Cafés: Grab a coffee or cocktail at Terraço Santa Luzia or Portas do Sol Café while admiring the view.

3. Miradouro da Graça (Sophia de Mello Breyner Andresen Viewpoint)

Located a bit further from Alfama, but still within walking distance, Miradouro da Graça offers a spectacular view of São Jorge Castle and downtown Lisbon.

- Why Visit?
  - Offers a less touristy, more relaxed atmosphere.
  - Features an outdoor café where visitors can enjoy drinks with a view.
  - One of the best places to see the sunset over Lisbon.
- How to Get There: A short uphill walk from Alfama or by Tram 28.

Tips for Exploring Alfama & Its Miradouros

- Wear Comfortable Shoes: Alfama's streets are steep and cobbled, so comfortable footwear is essential.
- Explore at a Slow Pace: The best way to experience Alfama is by getting lost in its winding streets.
- Visit in the Morning or Evening: The soft light at sunrise or sunset makes the views even more magical.
- Enjoy Local Cafés & Fado Music: Alfama is home to authentic Portuguese cafés and Fado houses where you can experience Portugal's traditional music.

Tram 28 & Iconic Lisbon Streets

Lisbon is a city where history, culture, and charm blend seamlessly, and nothing captures this essence better than the famous Tram 28 and its journey through the city's most iconic streets. This historic yellow tram has become a symbol of Lisbon, offering locals and tourists alike an unforgettable ride through the city's steep hills, winding alleyways, and breathtaking viewpoints. Along the route, passengers get to witness Lisbon's diverse neighborhoods, passing by ancient landmarks, bustling squares, and charming corners that make the city so unique.

Beyond Tram 28, Lisbon's streets themselves are attractions in their own right. From the picturesque lanes of Alfama to the grand boulevards of Baixa and the bohemian spirit of Bairro Alto, Lisbon's streets tell stories of its rich history, vibrant culture, and modern creativity.

The Legendary Tram 28: A Ride Through History

Tram 28 is not just a mode of transport; it is an experience that connects visitors with Lisbon's past and present. The iconic yellow tram, officially part of the Carris public transport system, has been operating since the early 20th century. It follows a picturesque and winding route that takes passengers through some of the city's most historic and scenic neighborhoods, including Graça, Alfama, Baixa, Chiado, and Estrela.

Why Is Tram 28 So Special?

- Historic Appeal: The tram uses vintage "Remodelado" trams from the 1930s, which retain their old-world charm with wooden interiors, brass fittings, and a nostalgic feel.
- Scenic Route: It passes through some of Lisbon's most famous landmarks, offering a mobile sightseeing experience.
- Affordable: A single ride on Tram 28 costs much less than a guided tour, making it one of the best-value ways to explore Lisbon.
- Perfect Photo Opportunities: The tram itself, along with the stunning backdrops of Lisbon's hills and architecture, makes for some of the most iconic Lisbon photographs.

The Tram 28 Route & Highlights
Tram 28 begins in Martim Moniz, a lively square at the heart of Lisbon, and ends in Campo de Ourique, a quiet and charming neighborhood. The full route covers 7 kilometers and takes about 40 minutes, though it can be longer during peak hours due to the tram's popularity.

Some of the most notable stops and sights along the way include:

- Graça: One of Lisbon's oldest neighborhoods, known for its miradouros (viewpoints), including the Miradouro da Senhora do Monte, which offers one of the best panoramic views of the city.
- Alfama: The heart of old Lisbon, filled with narrow alleys, Fado music, and traditional tiled houses. The tram winds through the district's labyrinthine streets, passing by the Sé Cathedral, São Jorge Castle, and charming local cafés.
- Baixa: The flat, structured downtown area featuring Praça do Comércio, Rossio Square, and Rua Augusta, where visitors can explore elegant architecture, historic shops, and bustling markets.
- Chiado: A sophisticated and artistic district filled with bookstores, theaters, and trendy cafés. This area has been a meeting place for writers, poets, and intellectuals for centuries.
- Bairro Alto: By day, it's a quiet residential area with colorful facades and hidden courtyards, but by night, it transforms into Lisbon's most famous nightlife hub.
- Estrela: Home to the beautiful Basilica da Estrela and the Jardim da Estrela, a peaceful public garden ideal for a break from the busy streets.
- Campo de Ourique: A charming residential neighborhood with a relaxed atmosphere and excellent local eateries, including the Mercado de Campo de Ourique.

Tips for Riding Tram 28

- Go Early or Late: The tram is incredibly popular, especially during peak tourist seasons. The best time to ride without long queues is early in the morning or late in the evening.
- Beware of Pickpockets: Due to the tram's popularity and crowded conditions, pickpockets often target passengers. Keep an eye on your belongings.

- Get a Viva Viagem Card: Instead of paying for a single ride, tourists can purchase a rechargeable Viva Viagem card, which allows for unlimited rides on public transport for 24 hours.
- Be Patient: Tram 28 is small and fills up quickly, meaning that visitors may have to wait for multiple trams before finding a seat.

Lisbon's Most Iconic Streets

Beyond the journey of Tram 28, Lisbon's streets themselves are part of its magic. Each district has a unique character, and exploring these streets on foot allows visitors to soak in the atmosphere, discover hidden gems, and experience the city like a local.

1. Rua Augusta (Baixa District)

Rua Augusta is Lisbon's grandest pedestrian street, stretching from Rossio Square to Praça do Comércio. It is lined with historic buildings, outdoor cafés, and street performers, creating a lively and vibrant atmosphere.

Highlights:

- Arco da Rua Augusta: A majestic triumphal arch at the entrance to Praça do Comércio, offering a viewing platform with panoramic city views.
- Traditional Shops: Rua Augusta is home to century-old bakeries, souvenir shops, and upscale boutiques.

2. Rua Garrett (Chiado District)

Rua Garrett is the heart of Chiado, Lisbon's elegant and literary quarter. It is a street that blends historical charm with modern shopping and cultural attractions.

Highlights:

- Livraria Bertrand: Recognized as the world's oldest operating bookstore, dating back to 1732.
- Café A Brasileira: A historic café where Portugal's most famous poet, Fernando Pessoa, used to frequent.

3. Rua da Bica de Duarte Belo (Bica District)
This picturesque street is one of the most photographed in Lisbon, thanks to its steep incline, pastel-colored buildings, and the famous yellow funicular, Elevador da Bica.

Highlights:

- Bica Funicular: A historic cable car that has been operating since 1892, offering a classic Lisbon postcard scene.
- Trendy Bars and Cafés: The Bica district is full of hidden taverns and modern cocktail bars, perfect for an evening out.

4. Avenida da Liberdade (Luxury & Elegance)
This broad, tree-lined boulevard is Lisbon's most luxurious street, often compared to Paris's Champs-Élysées. It is lined with designer shops, five-star hotels, and elegant theaters.

Highlights:

- Luxury Shopping: Home to brands like Louis Vuitton, Gucci, and Prada.
- Cinemateca Portuguesa: A historic cinema showcasing classic Portuguese films.

5. Calçada Portuguesa Streets (Lisbon's Mosaic Pavements)
One of Lisbon's most defining features is its "calçada portuguesa", or Portuguese mosaic sidewalks. These artistic cobblestone patterns are found throughout the city, particularly in Baixa, Chiado, and Avenida da Liberdade.

Highlights:

- Rossio Square's Wave Patterns: A famous example of calçada art, giving the illusion of movement.
- Chiado's Nautical Motifs: Inspired by Portugal's seafaring history.

Praça do Comércio & Baixa District

Lisbon's Praça do Comércio and the Baixa district are at the heart of the city's historical and cultural identity. As one of the most recognizable landmarks in Portugal, Praça do Comércio (also known as Terreiro do Paço) is a grand riverside square symbolizing Lisbon's rich maritime heritage. Meanwhile, Baixa is the city's downtown area, known for its elegant neoclassical architecture, bustling streets, and vibrant commercial scene. This area is a must-visit for anyone exploring Lisbon, as it offers a mix of history, culture, shopping, dining, and iconic sights.

Praça do Comércio: Lisbon's Grand Riverside Square

Praça do Comércio is one of the largest and most beautiful squares in Europe, sitting along the banks of the Tagus River. It was originally the site of the Royal Ribeira Palace, which was destroyed in the 1755 earthquake. Following the disaster, the square was redesigned as an open public space, becoming the political and commercial heart of Lisbon. Today, it remains one of the city's most significant landmarks.

Key Features of Praça do Comércio
1. Arco da Rua Augusta (Rua Augusta Arch)

One of the most striking features of the square is the Arco da Rua Augusta, a monumental arch that marks the entrance to Rua Augusta, Baixa's main street. This neoclassical arch was built to celebrate Lisbon's reconstruction after the earthquake.

- Visitors can climb to the top of the arch for panoramic views over Praça do Comércio, the Tagus River, and downtown Lisbon.
- The arch is adorned with sculptures of historical figures, including Vasco da Gama, the Marquis of Pombal, and Nuno Álvares Pereira.

2. Equestrian Statue of King José I

101

At the center of the square stands a bronze statue of King José I, who was Portugal's ruler during the earthquake. The statue depicts the king on horseback, with his horse trampling serpents, symbolizing his leadership in overcoming the disaster.

3. Cais das Colunas (Columns of the Pier)

Facing the river, visitors will find two ornamental columns, which were once part of the royal entrance to the city. This area, known as Cais das Colunas, is a popular spot for sitting by the water, enjoying the breeze, and watching the ferries cross the river.

4. Museums & Government Buildings

The grand yellow buildings that surround the square house various government offices, restaurants, and cultural institutions. The Lisbon Story Centre, located here, offers an interactive exhibition on Lisbon's history, including the 1755 earthquake and its aftermath.

Things to Do in Praça do Comércio

- Take photos of the stunning architecture and riverfront views.
- Climb the Rua Augusta Arch for breathtaking city views.
- Visit the Lisbon Story Centre to learn about the city's history.
- Relax at Cais das Colunas and enjoy the scenic riverfront.
- Dine at a terrace café while watching the city's vibrant energy.

Exploring the Baixa District: The Heart of Lisbon

Baixa, meaning "low" in Portuguese, is Lisbon's downtown district. It was completely rebuilt after the 1755 earthquake under the direction of the Marquis of Pombal, giving it its distinctive grid-like street layout and neoclassical architecture. Today, Baixa is a hub for shopping, dining, and sightseeing.

1. Rua Augusta: The Main Pedestrian Street

Running from Praça do Comércio to Rossio Square, Rua Augusta is Lisbon's most famous pedestrian street. It is lined with shops, cafés, and restaurants, making it a lively place for a stroll.

- Visitors will find traditional Portuguese souvenir shops, international brands, and charming street performers along the way.
- The patterned mosaic pavement of Rua Augusta is an example of Portuguese "calçada" stonework, a feature seen throughout Lisbon.

2. Elevador de Santa Justa (Santa Justa Lift)

One of Baixa's most iconic landmarks, the Santa Justa Lift, connects Baixa with the higher district of Carmo.

- Designed by Raoul Mesnier de Ponsard, an apprentice of Gustave Eiffel, the lift resembles the engineering style of the Eiffel Tower.
- Visitors can ride the elevator to the top for spectacular views of the city.

3. Praça Dom Pedro IV (Rossio Square)

Just north of Baixa, Rossio Square is one of the city's most historic and vibrant squares.

- The square features wave-patterned pavement, a common design in Portuguese cities.
- It is home to the National Theatre D. Maria II and the Baroque-style Rossio Train Station, one of the most beautiful train stations in Portugal.

4. Praça da Figueira

Another key square in Baixa, Praça da Figueira is known for its traditional market atmosphere.

- The square hosts local food stalls and bakeries, making it a great place to try pastéis de nata (custard tarts).
- A statue of King João I on horseback stands at the center.

5. Convento do Carmo (Carmo Convent)
A short walk from Santa Justa Lift, Carmo Convent is one of Lisbon's most fascinating historic sites.

- The convent was destroyed in the 1755 earthquake, and its roofless Gothic arches now serve as a reminder of the disaster.
- Today, the site houses the Carmo Archaeological Museum, displaying artifacts from different periods of Lisbon's history.

Dining & Shopping in Baixa
Baixa is one of the best places in Lisbon to experience traditional Portuguese cuisine and do some shopping.

1. Best Places to Eat in Baixa

- Cervejaria Ramiro – Famous for its seafood dishes, including garlic prawns and king crab.
- Café Nicola – A historic café that dates back to the 18th century, known for its strong espresso and pastries.
- A Ginginha – A small bar where visitors can try ginjinha, a traditional cherry liqueur.
- Time Out Market (near Cais do Sodré) – A food hall featuring stalls from some of Lisbon's best chefs.

2. Best Shopping Streets in Baixa

- Rua Augusta – The main shopping street with a mix of fashion boutiques, souvenir shops, and international brands.
- Rua do Ouro & Rua da Prata – Historically known for Lisbon's gold and silver workshops, now home to jewelry stores and classic Portuguese shops.
- Conserveira de Lisboa – A famous shop specializing in beautifully packaged canned fish, a unique Lisbon souvenir.

Why Praça do Comércio & Baixa Are Must-Visit Destinations

- Historical Significance: The area represents Lisbon's resilience and rebirth after the 1755 earthquake.
- Architectural Beauty: From the grand neoclassical buildings to the intricate Portuguese pavement designs, every corner of Baixa is visually stunning.
- Central Location: It is within walking distance of many other major attractions, making it an ideal starting point for exploring Lisbon.
- Great for Shopping & Dining: Baixa offers a mix of traditional markets, modern boutiques, historic cafés, and gourmet restaurants.
- Riverside Ambiance: Praça do Comércio provides a relaxing waterfront setting where visitors can enjoy the beauty of the Tagus River.

LX Factory: The Hipster Paradise

Introduction to LX Factory

Nestled beneath the 25 de Abril Bridge, in the Alcântara district of Lisbon, LX Factory is a creative hub, cultural hotspot, and urban oasis that has transformed an old industrial complex into one of the city's trendiest destinations. Originally a 19th-century textile factory, the space has been repurposed into a vibrant community of artists, entrepreneurs, food lovers, and independent businesses.

LX Factory is a blend of past and present, where industrial-era buildings are covered in colorful street art, warehouses have been turned into stylish cafés and boutiques, and former factory spaces now host bookstores, art galleries, and rooftop bars. This dynamic space is where Lisbon's creative energy thrives, making it a must-visit for travelers looking for something beyond traditional tourist sites.

A Brief History of LX Factory

Before LX Factory became Lisbon's hipster paradise, it had a long history as an industrial complex. Built in 1846, the space was originally home to Companhia de Fiação e Tecidos Lisbonense, one of Portugal's largest textile manufacturers. Over the years, the complex housed various industries, including printing presses and food processing plants, before falling into neglect in the late 20th century.

In 2008, a group of visionaries saw potential in the abandoned factory buildings and launched a project to revitalize the area. Their goal was to create a modern, creative hub while preserving the historic character of the site. Today, LX Factory is a symbol of Lisbon's cultural revival, drawing visitors from around the world with its unique atmosphere and ever-evolving artistic scene.

What to See & Do at LX Factory

1. Explore the Street Art & Murals: One of the first things visitors notice when they arrive at LX Factory is the **impressive street art covering nearly every surface**. The walls, doors, and even staircases are **adorned with vibrant murals, thought-provoking graffiti, and large-scale installations** created by both local and international artists.

Some standout artworks include:

- A massive mural of a watchful eye by Portuguese street artist Vhils, known for his technique of carving into walls.
- Playful, surreal illustrations by artist Bordalo II, who creates eco-conscious pieces using recycled materials.

- Colorful geometric designs and abstract art that give LX Factory its distinctive urban feel.

Walking through the complex feels like strolling through an open-air art gallery, where every turn reveals a new masterpiece waiting to be discovered.

2. Visit Ler Devagar: The Most Iconic Bookstore: One of LX Factory's most famous spots is **Ler Devagar (which means "Read Slowly" in Portuguese)**, a **stunning independent bookstore** housed in a former printing press. The high-ceilinged space is lined with towering bookshelves, and an old **printing machine still sits at the center of the store**, adding to its historical charm.

Beyond books, Ler Devagar also serves as a cultural venue, frequently hosting literary events, live music performances, and art exhibitions. Even for those who don't plan on buying a book, the atmosphere alone makes it worth a visit.

3. Discover Unique Shops & Boutiques: LX Factory is home to **some of the quirkiest and most creative shops in Lisbon**, offering everything from handmade crafts to high-end designer pieces. Some highlights include:

- The Folks – A store specializing in Portuguese-made products, from ceramics and textiles to gourmet food and wines.
- Organii Bio – A boutique selling eco-friendly and organic beauty products.
- Rutz – A unique shop that sells shoes made from sustainable cork, one of Portugal's signature materials.

Shopping at LX Factory is about more than just buying souvenirs—it's about discovering innovative, locally crafted goods that reflect Lisbon's creative spirit.

4. Enjoy a Coffee or Pastry at an Artsy Café: The cafés at LX Factory are as **aesthetically pleasing as they are delicious**, offering visitors a perfect place to relax and soak in the creative atmosphere. Some of the best spots include:

- Wish Slow Coffee House – A cozy café with specialty coffee, homemade cakes, and a laid-back vibe.
- Montana Lisboa Café – A graffiti-inspired café that doubles as an art supply store, perfect for urban art lovers.
- Café na Fábrica – Located in an old factory space, this café is famous for its delicious brunch menu and artistic decor.

Whether visitors want to sip on a locally roasted espresso, indulge in a pastel de nata, or try an alternative brunch, LX Factory's café scene does not disappoint.

5. Experience Rooftop Views & Cocktails: No visit to LX Factory is complete without a drink at **Rio Maravilha**, a rooftop bar and restaurant with **breathtaking views of the Tagus River and the 25 de Abril Bridge**. The venue combines **bright, playful decor with an excellent cocktail menu**, making it an ideal spot to watch the sunset over Lisbon.

For those looking for a more laid-back experience, LX Rooftop Bar is another great choice, offering chill vibes, live DJ sets, and refreshing sangria.

6. Indulge in LX Factory's Food Scene: LX Factory is home to **some of Lisbon's most exciting restaurants**, offering a mix of

traditional Portuguese cuisine and international flavors. Some must-try spots include:

- Cantina LX – One of the original restaurants in LX Factory, serving traditional Portuguese dishes in a rustic, industrial setting.
- 1300 Taberna – A creative fine-dining restaurant known for its innovative takes on Portuguese classics.
- Pizzaria Lisboa – A popular spot for authentic Italian-style pizzas made with fresh, local ingredients.

With so many options to choose from, food lovers will find themselves spoiled for choice at LX Factory.

Events & Nightlife at LX Factory

Beyond its daytime attractions, LX Factory comes alive at night with a variety of events, concerts, and parties. The complex frequently hosts:

- Live music performances featuring local and international artists.
- Art exhibitions and pop-up galleries, showcasing Lisbon's vibrant creative scene.
- Themed markets and craft fairs, where visitors can discover handmade goods and vintage treasures.

For those looking for a laid-back but lively nightlife scene, LX Factory is the perfect place to enjoy live music, craft cocktails, and a buzzing atmosphere without the intensity of Lisbon's bigger clubs.

111

How to Get to LX Factory

LX Factory is located in Alcântara, about halfway between central Lisbon and the district of Belém. There are several ways to reach it:

- By Tram – Take Tram 15E from Praça da Figueira or Cais do Sodré.
- By Bus – Several buses, including 714 and 727, stop near LX Factory.
- By Train – Take a train from Cais do Sodré to Alcântara-Mar Station, then walk a few minutes to the complex.
- By Taxi or Ride-Sharing – Uber and Bolt rides are affordable and convenient options.

Day Trips: Sintra, Cascais & Beyond

Lisbon is an extraordinary city filled with charm, but its surroundings offer equally mesmerizing landscapes, historic palaces, and beautiful coastal towns that are well worth a visit. Among the most popular day trips from Lisbon, Sintra and Cascais stand out as must-visit destinations. However, there are also lesser-known gems, such as Arrábida Natural Park, Óbidos, and Évora, that provide unique cultural and natural experiences.

This chapter explores the best day trips from Lisbon, detailing what makes each location special and how to get there for an unforgettable experience.

1. Sintra – The Fairytale Town of Portugal

Why Visit Sintra?

Sintra is a UNESCO-listed town nestled in the lush hills of the Sintra-Cascais Natural Park. Known for its romantic palaces, exotic gardens, and mystical atmosphere, Sintra has captivated travelers for centuries, including writers like Lord Byron, who called it a "glorious Eden."

Top Attractions in Sintra

- Palácio da Pena (Pena Palace)

    o A colorful, Disney-like palace perched on a hilltop, offering spectacular panoramic views.
    o Features Neo-Gothic, Neo-Renaissance, and Moorish influences, making it one of Europe's most unique palaces.

- o   Tip: Arrive early to avoid crowds and explore the surrounding Parque da Pena, a stunning forested park with hidden trails.
- Castelo dos Mouros (Moorish Castle)

  - o   An ancient 8th-century fortress built by the Moors, offering breathtaking views of Sintra and the Atlantic Ocean.
  - o   Visitors can walk along the stone walls and towers for a medieval adventure.
- Palácio Nacional de Sintra (National Palace of Sintra)

  - o   A well-preserved medieval royal palace in the heart of Sintra, recognizable by its two iconic conical chimneys.
  - o   The interior features beautiful Azulejo tiles and grand halls used by Portuguese kings.
- Quinta da Regaleira

  - o   A magical estate filled with hidden tunnels, mystical wells, and mysterious symbols.
  - o   The Initiation Well, an underground spiral staircase, is a highlight that intrigues visitors with its ties to Freemasonry and alchemy.
- Palácio de Monserrate

  - o   A lesser-visited yet stunning palace with a blend of Moorish, Gothic, and Indian architectural styles.
  - o   Surrounded by lush botanical gardens with rare plants from around the world.

How to Get to Sintra

- By Train: The most convenient way is by train from Lisbon's Rossio Station, taking around 40 minutes.

- By Car: A 30-minute drive, but parking is limited in Sintra's historic center.
- By Tour: Many guided day trips from Lisbon include Sintra's top attractions, often combined with Cascais.

2. Cascais – The Stylish Seaside Escape

Why Visit Cascais?
Located just 30 km west of Lisbon, Cascais is a charming coastal town known for its golden beaches, stylish marina, and elegant villas. Once a fishing village, it became a retreat for Portuguese royalty and is now one of the most sophisticated destinations near Lisbon.

Top Attractions in Cascais
- Praia do Guincho

- One of the best surfing beaches in Portugal, featuring strong waves and golden sand dunes.
- Popular with both surfers and nature lovers due to its wild and scenic landscape.

- Boca do Inferno (Hell's Mouth)

  - A dramatic sea cliff formation where waves crash into caves and tunnels.
  - Best visited during sunset for spectacular ocean views.

- Cascais Marina & Historic Center

  - A picturesque area with charming cafés, boutique shops, and seafood restaurants.
  - The Marina de Cascais is filled with luxury yachts and offers a relaxed seaside atmosphere.

- Palácio da Cidadela de Cascais

  - A historic fortress-turned-palace that once housed Portuguese royalty.
  - Features art galleries, exhibitions, and a peaceful courtyard.

- Museu Condes de Castro Guimarães

  - A 19th-century palace-turned-museum, showcasing antique furniture, art collections, and a library.
  - Surrounded by beautiful gardens and set next to a small beach.

How to Get to Cascais

- By Train: A scenic train ride from Lisbon's Cais do Sodré Station takes around 40 minutes along the coastline.
- By Car: A 35-minute drive via the Marginal Road, which offers stunning ocean views.

- By Bike: Rent a bike and cycle along the coastal Cascais-Estoril promenade, a beautiful route connecting Lisbon and Cascais.

3. Arrábida Natural Park – A Hidden Coastal Paradise

Why Visit Arrábida?

For those seeking pristine beaches, lush mountains, and turquoise waters, Arrábida Natural Park is a hidden gem located 40 km south of Lisbon. This protected area is perfect for hiking, snorkeling, and beach relaxation.

Top Attractions in Arrábida

Praia da Galapinhos

Often ranked as one of Europe's most beautiful beaches, with crystal-clear waters and white sand.

Serra da Arrábida

Offers breathtaking hiking trails through Mediterranean forests and limestone cliffs.

Setúbal & Portinho da Arrábida

Visit the charming fishing town of Setúbal, famous for its fresh seafood and dolphin-watching tours.

How to Get to Arrábida

By Car: The best way to explore Arrábida is by rental car, as public transport is limited.

By Tour: Several guided tours offer hiking, wine tasting, and beach visits in Arrábida.

4. Óbidos – The Enchanting Medieval Village

Why Visit Óbidos?

Óbidos is a well-preserved medieval town, famous for its whitewashed houses, cobbled streets, and castle walls. Walking through Óbidos feels like stepping back in time.

Top Attractions in Óbidos

Óbidos Castle

A 12th-century fortress that now serves as a hotel.

Rua Direita

The main street filled with charming shops, cafés, and bookstores.

Ginjinha de Óbidos

Taste the famous cherry liqueur served in chocolate cups.

How to Get to Óbidos

By Bus: From Lisbon's Campo Grande station, taking about 1 hour.

By Car: A 1-hour drive via the A8 highway.

5. Évora – The City of History & Culture

Why Visit Évora?

A UNESCO World Heritage city, Évora is one of Portugal's most historically significant towns, with Roman and medieval landmarks.

Top Attractions in Évora
Temple of Diana
A Roman temple from the 1st century, one of Portugal's best-preserved ruins.
Capela dos Ossos (Chapel of Bones)
A macabre yet fascinating chapel lined with human skulls and bones.
Évora Cathedral

A magnificent Gothic cathedral offering panoramic views from its rooftop.

How to Get to Évora

By Train: Around 1.5 hours from Lisbon's Entrecampos Station.

By Car: A 90-minute drive via the A6 highway.

Chapter 5

Must-Try Portuguese Dishes (Bacalhau, Pastéis de Nata, etc.)

Lisbon's culinary scene is a vibrant mix of fresh seafood, rich pastries, flavorful stews, and bold wines, influenced by Portugal's maritime history and cultural heritage. The city's cuisine reflects a perfect blend of traditional recipes, Mediterranean flavors, and global influences from Portugal's former colonies, including Brazil, Mozambique, and Goa. Whether you're savoring a plate of Bacalhau à Brás in a cozy tasca or enjoying a warm Pastel de Nata at a historic café, Lisbon offers a delightful gastronomic journey that every visitor should experience.

This chapter highlights the must-try Portuguese dishes in Lisbon, their cultural significance, and where to find the best versions of these classic delights.

1. Bacalhau – The Iconic Portuguese Codfish

Why is Bacalhau So Important?

Bacalhau, or salted cod, is Portugal's national dish, with over 365 different recipes—one for each day of the year. This dish is a legacy of Portugal's maritime explorations, as sailors would preserve cod by salting it for long voyages. Today, it is a staple in Portuguese cuisine, appearing in various forms on restaurant menus across Lisbon.

Must-Try Bacalhau Dishes in Lisbon

Bacalhau à Brás

One of Lisbon's most beloved bacalhau dishes, featuring shredded codfish stir-fried with onions, straw fries, eggs, garlic, and parsley.

Where to Try It: O Velho Eurico (Alfama) and Laurentina – O Rei do Bacalhau.

Bacalhau com Natas

A creamy and indulgent dish made with salted cod, onions, potatoes, and baked in a rich béchamel sauce.

Where to Try It: A Casa do Bacalhau and Restaurante Zé da Mouraria.

Bacalhau à Lagareiro

A simple yet flavorful dish where cod is grilled or roasted and served with olive oil, roasted potatoes, and garlic.

Where to Try It: Ramiro (Baixa) and Solar dos Presuntos.

2. Pastéis de Nata – The Famous Portuguese Custard Tarts

What Makes Pastéis de Nata Special?

Pastéis de Nata, or Portuguese custard tarts, are Lisbon's most famous pastry. These crispy, flaky tarts filled with creamy egg custard have a caramelized top, making them irresistibly delicious. They were originally created by monks at the Jerónimos Monastery in Belém in the 18th century.

Where to Find the Best Pastéis de Nata in Lisbon

Pastéis de Belém (Belém) – The original bakery since 1837, known for its secret recipe.

Manteigaria (Chiado & Time Out Market) – A local favorite, famous for its perfectly crispy and caramelized tarts.

Fábrica da Nata (Restauradores & Baixa) – Serves freshly baked tarts throughout the day with a velvety custard filling.

3. Sardinhas Assadas – Grilled Sardines

Why Are Sardines a Lisbon Staple?

Grilled sardines are a summertime favorite in Lisbon, especially during the Festas de Santo António in June, when the streets are filled with the smell of charcoal-grilled fish. Sardines are simply seasoned with coarse salt, grilled over open flames, and served with bread, roasted peppers, and salad.

Where to Eat the Best Sardines in Lisbon

Páteo 13 (Alfama) – A hidden gem serving freshly grilled sardines in a lively outdoor setting.

Casa do Alentejo (Baixa) – Offers traditional grilled sardines with authentic Portuguese sides.

Zé dos Cornos (Mouraria) – A rustic tasca known for affordable and perfectly cooked sardines.

4. Polvo à Lagareiro – Octopus with Olive Oil & Garlic

This dish is a seafood lover's dream, featuring tender octopus roasted with garlic, olive oil, and potatoes. It is one of the most flavorful and popular seafood dishes in Lisbon.

Where to Try It:

Ramiro (Intendente) – A seafood institution serving delicious octopus dishes.

A Cevicheria (Príncipe Real) – Offers a modern twist on traditional seafood plates.

5. Prego – Portugal's Iconic Sandwiches.

Prego (Beef Sandwich)

The beef counterpart of the bifana, typically served in soft bread with garlic butter.

Where to Try It: Prego da Peixaria (Cais do Sodré) – A modern take on the classic prego sandwich.

6. Caldo Verde – The Beloved Portuguese Soup

What is Caldo Verde?

Traditional Portuguese soup made with kale, potatoes, onions, and chorizo, often enjoyed as a comforting dish during the colder months.

Where to Try It:

Solar dos Presuntos (Avenida da Liberdade) – Serves one of the best caldo verde soups in Lisbon.

7. Arroz de Marisco – Portuguese Seafood Rice

This dish is Portugal's answer to paella—a rich, flavorful seafood rice dish made with shrimp, clams, mussels, and aromatic spices.

Where to Try It:

Marisqueira Uma (Baixa) – A famous spot for authentic arroz de marisco.

Best Restaurants for Every Budget

Lisbon's food scene is a vibrant reflection of Portugal's rich culinary heritage. From traditional seafood dishes to modern fusion cuisine, the city offers an array of dining experiences catering to every budget. Whether you're a budget-conscious traveler, a mid-range foodie, or someone looking for a luxurious gourmet meal, Lisbon has something for everyone.

This chapter explores the best restaurants in Lisbon across different price ranges, ensuring that no matter what your budget is, you can experience the city's incredible food culture.

Budget-Friendly Restaurants (€)

For travelers who want to enjoy authentic Portuguese cuisine without breaking the bank, Lisbon has many affordable eateries that serve delicious, hearty meals at reasonable prices.

1. Cervejaria Ramiro

Address: Av. Alm. Reis 1 H, 1150-007 Lisboa, Portugal

Specialty: Seafood

Why Visit?: This legendary seafood restaurant is famous for its garlic butter prawns, clams, and lobster. The food is fresh, the portions are generous, and the prices are reasonable for the quality.

Must-Try: Order the prego (steak sandwich) after your seafood feast—it's a local tradition.

Contact: +351 969 839 472

Menu-Website: thefork.pt

2. Zé da Mouraria

Address : R. João do Outeiro 24, 1100-292 Lisbon, Portugal

Specialty: Bacalhau (salt cod) dishes

Why Visit?: One of the best places to experience traditional Portuguese home cooking at a great price. The portions are huge, making it perfect for sharing.

Must-Try: Their Bacalhau à Brás, a comforting dish made with shredded cod, eggs, and potatoes.

Contact : +351 21 886 5436

3. O Trevo

Address : 1200-283 Lisbon, Portugal

Specialty: Bifana (pork sandwich)

Why Visit?: A small but iconic local café where you can enjoy one of the best bifanas in Lisbon. This simple pork sandwich, seasoned with garlic and spices, is a must-try street food item.

Must-Try: A bifana with mustard and a cold beer—a true Lisbon experience.

Contact : +351 21 346 8092

Menu-website: digitalmenucheck.com

Mid-Range Restaurants (€€)

For those who want an elevated dining experience without spending a fortune, Lisbon has a great selection of mid-range restaurants that balance quality and affordability.

1. Taberna da Rua das Flores

Address: Rua das Flores 103 109, 1200-194 Lisboa, Portugal

Specialty: Creative Portuguese small plates

Why Visit?: This charming taberna offers an inventive menu inspired by traditional Portuguese flavors with a modern twist. The dishes are perfect for sharing, making it a great spot for a group meal.

Must-Try: The octopus rice with coriander and the pork cheek stew.

Service options: Cash only · Doesn't accept reservations · Dogs allowed

2. Bairro do Avillez

Address: R. Nova da Trindade 18, 1200-303 Lisboa, Portugal

Specialty: Contemporary Portuguese cuisine

Why Visit?: Created by Michelin-starred chef José Avillez, this restaurant is divided into different sections, including a taberna, a seafood counter, and a fine dining area.

Must-Try: The piri-piri chicken or the roasted suckling pig sandwich.

Phone: +351 21 583 0290

Menu-Website: bairrodoavillez.pt

3. A Cevicheria

Address: R. Dom Pedro V 129, 1250-096 Lisboa, Portugal

Specialty: Peruvian and Portuguese fusion seafood

Why Visit?: This restaurant by chef Kiko Martins specializes in ceviche and seafood dishes with Portuguese flavors. The massive octopus sculpture hanging from the ceiling adds to the stylish ambiance.

Must-Try: The Lisbon ceviche, made with codfish and lupin beans.

Phone: +351 21 803 8815

Menu-Website: acevicheria.pt

High-End & Fine Dining Restaurants (€€€-€€€€)

For those looking to splurge on a luxurious meal, Lisbon has an impressive selection of Michelin-starred and gourmet restaurants that showcase Portuguese cuisine at its finest.

1. Belcanto (2 Michelin Stars)

Address: R. Serpa Pinto 10A, 1200-026 Lisboa, Portugal

Specialty: Fine dining Portuguese cuisine

Why Visit?: One of Portugal's most celebrated restaurants, led by chef José Avillez. Offers an exceptional tasting menu that blends traditional Portuguese flavors with contemporary techniques.

Must-Try: The Carabineiro (scarlet prawn) with seaweed butter.

Contact: +351 21 342 0607

Menu-Website: belcanto.pt

2. Alma (2 Michelin Stars)

Address : R. Anchieta 15, 1200-224 Lisbon, Portugal

Specialty: Modern Portuguese haute cuisine

Why Visit?: A sophisticated yet relaxed restaurant that serves meticulously crafted dishes inspired by both Portugal and global flavors.

Must-Try: The tasting menu, featuring dishes like suckling pig with smoked eel.

Contact: +351 21 347 0650

Menu-Website: almalisboa.pt

3. Feitoria (1 Michelin Star)

Address: Altis Belem Hotel & Spa, Doca do Bom Sucesso, 1400-038 Lisboa, Portugal

Specialty: Innovative Portuguese cuisine

Why Visit?: A refined dining experience with a strong emphasis on sustainable, locally sourced ingredients.

Must-Try: The tasting menu with wine pairing.

Contact: +351 21 040 0208

Menu-Website: restaurantefeitoria.com

4. Loco (1 Michelin Star)

Address : R. Navegantes nº53-B, 1200-731 Lisbon, Portugal

Specialty: Avant-garde tasting menus

Why Visit?: This experimental restaurant offers a 20-course tasting menu that surprises guests with creative presentations.

Must-Try: The chef's seasonal menu, which changes frequently.

Contact: +351 21 395 1861

Menu-Website: loco.pt

Famous Cafés & Local Bakeries

Lisbon's rich culinary heritage is deeply intertwined with its vibrant café culture and renowned bakeries. From historic establishments that have stood the test of time to modern spots pushing the boundaries of pastry arts, the city offers a plethora of venues where locals and visitors alike can indulge in delectable treats and aromatic coffees. Below is a curated selection of some of Lisbon's most iconic cafés and bakeries, complete with their addresses, contact information, and websites where available.

1. A Brasileira

Address: Rua Garrett 120-122, 1200-205 Lisbon, Portugal
Contact: +351 213 469 541
Website: www.abrasileira.pt

Established in 1905, A Brasileira is one of Lisbon's most historic cafés. Located in the heart of the Chiado district, it is famed for its Art Deco interior and as a former haunt of intellectuals and artists, including the celebrated poet Fernando Pessoa, whose bronze statue adorns the entrance.

2. Pastéis de Belém

Address: Rua de Belém 84-92, 1300-085 Lisbon, Portugal
Contact: +351 213 637 423
Website: www.pasteisdebelem.pt

Since 1837, Pastéis de Belém has been delighting patrons with its secret-recipe custard tarts, known as "pastéis de nata." Located near the Jerónimos Monastery in the Belém district, this bakery is a must-visit for anyone seeking an authentic taste of Lisbon's most famous pastry.

3. Confeitaria Nacional

Address: Praça da Figueira 18B, 1100-241 Lisbon, Portugal
Contact: +351 213 424 470
Website: www.confeitarianacional.com

Founded in 1829, Confeitaria Nacional is one of the oldest pastry shops in Lisbon. Situated in the Baixa district, it is renowned for its traditional Portuguese confections, including the "Bolo Rei" (King Cake), a staple during the Christmas season.

4. Manteigaria

Address: Rua do Loreto 2, 1200-108 Lisbon, Portugal
Contact: +351 213 471 492
Website: www.manteigaria.com

Manteigaria has quickly become a favorite among locals and tourists for its exceptional pastéis de nata. Located in the bustling Bairro Alto neighborhood, the bakery offers a modern take on the classic custard tart, with an open kitchen allowing visitors to watch the baking process.

5. Fabrica Coffee Roasters

Address: Rua das Portas de Santo Antão 136, 1150-269 Lisbon,
Portugal
Contact: +351 213 471 355
Website: www.fabricacoffeeroasters.com

For coffee enthusiasts, Fabrica Coffee Roasters provides a
contemporary café experience with a focus on specialty brews.
With multiple locations across the city, including one near Avenida
da Liberdade, it offers a cozy atmosphere to enjoy freshly roasted
coffee and light bites.

6. Café Martinho da Arcada

Address: Praça do Comércio 3, 1100-148 Lisbon, Portugal
Contact: +351 218 879 259
Website: www.martinhodaarcada.pt

Opened in 1782, Martinho da Arcada is the oldest café in Lisbon.
Located in the iconic Praça do Comércio, it has been frequented by
notable figures such as Fernando Pessoa, whose presence is
commemorated within. The café offers a traditional Portuguese
menu alongside its historic charm.

7. Pastelaria Versailles

Address: Avenida da República 15A, 1050-185 Lisbon, Portugal
Contact: +351 213 546 340
Website: www.pastelariaversailles.com

Since 1922, Pastelaria Versailles has been enchanting visitors with
its opulent interior and wide array of pastries. Located in the

Areeiro district, this elegant café is known for its exquisite cakes, savory snacks, and a selection of fine teas and coffees.

8. Fábrica da Nata

Address: Praça dos Restauradores 62-68, 1250-188 Lisbon, Portugal
Contact: +351 210 534 649
Website: www.fabricadanata.com

Specializing in the iconic pastéis de nata, Fábrica da Nata offers a modern setting where guests can enjoy freshly baked custard tarts accompanied by a variety of beverages. Its central location near Restauradores Square makes it a convenient stop for a sweet treat.

9. Café Nicola

Address: Praça Dom Pedro IV 24-25, 1100-200 Lisbon, Portugal
Contact: +351 213 460 486
Website: www.cafenicola.pt

Café Nicola, established in the 18th century, is a historic café situated in Rossio Square. Known for its literary connections, it was a popular meeting spot for writers and artists. Today, it continues to serve a range of traditional Portuguese dishes and pastries in a classic ambiance.

10. Padaria Portuguesa

Address: Multiple locations across Lisbon
Contact: Varies by location
Website: www.apadariaportuguesa.pt

A popular bakery chain in Lisbon, Padaria Portuguesa offers a wide selection of breads, pastries, and sandwiches. With numerous outlets throughout the city, it provides a convenient option for those seeking quality baked goods and a casual dining experience.

11. Landeau Chocolate

Address: Rua das Flores 70, 1200-195 Lisbon, Portugal
Contact: +351 915 953 271
Website: www.landeau.pt

Chocolate lovers should not miss Landeau Chocolate, famed for its indulgent chocolate cake, often hailed as one of the best in the world. With a minimalist interior, the focus remains on delivering a rich and memorable dessert experience.

12. Pastelaria Alçôa

Address: Rua Garrett 37, 1200-203 Lisbon, Portugal
Contact: +351 213 420 838
Website: www.alcoa.pt

Originating from the town of Alcobaça, Pastelaria Alcôa has brought its award-winning conventual pastries to Lisbon. Located in the Chiado district, it offers a range of traditional sweets, including the acclaimed.

Where to Find the Best Fado & Wine Bars

Lisbon's cultural landscape is deeply enriched by the soulful strains of Fado music and the robust flavors of Portuguese wines. To fully experience the city's heritage, visiting authentic Fado houses and distinguished wine bars is essential. Below is a curated selection of some of the finest establishments in Lisbon, complete with addresses, contact information, and websites where available.

Fado Restaurants

1. O Faia

Established in 1947 in the vibrant Bairro Alto district, O Faia offers a harmonious blend of traditional Fado performances and contemporary Portuguese cuisine. The menu emphasizes fresh, seasonal ingredients, ensuring a memorable dining experience.

- Address: Rua da Barroca 54-56, 1200-050 Lisbon
- Phone: +351 21 342 6742
- Website: https://www.ofaia.com/

2. Retiro dos Sentidos

Nestled in Bairro Alto, Retiro dos Sentidos captivates guests with its traditional décor, featuring shawls and terracotta dishes. The restaurant serves classic Portuguese dishes at reasonable prices, accompanied by authentic Fado performances.

- Address: Rua Diário de Notícias 62, 1200-145 Lisbon
- Phone: +351 21 343 6609
- Website: https://www.retirodossentidos.pt/

3. Duetos da Sé

Located near Lisbon Cathedral in Alfama, Duetos da Sé is a cultural hub offering live Fado performances alongside art exhibitions and book presentations. The venue combines gastronomy with culture, providing a unique experience for visitors.

- Address: Travessa do Almargem 1B, 1100-019 Lisbon
- Phone: +351 91 865 1266
- Website: https://www.duetosdase.com/

4. Café Luso

Situated in a former palace in Bairro Alto, Café Luso exudes elegance with its opulent interiors, including crystal chandeliers and ornate tilework. The restaurant offers a curated dining experience featuring traditional Portuguese delicacies accompanied by live Fado music.

- Address: Travessa da Queimada 10, 1200-365 Lisbon
- Phone: +351 21 342 2281
- Website: https://www.cafeluso.pt/

5. Tasca do Chico

A beloved institution in Bairro Alto, Tasca do Chico offers an intimate setting for Fado enthusiasts. The cozy atmosphere, coupled with heartfelt performances, makes it a favorite among locals and visitors alike.

- Address: Rua do Diário de Notícias 39, 1200-141 Lisbon
- Phone: +351 21 343 1048
- Website: https://www.facebook.com/tascadochico/

6. Parreirinha de Alfama

Located in the historic Alfama district, Parreirinha de Alfama is renowned for its authentic Fado performances and traditional Portuguese cuisine. The intimate setting and rich history make it a must-visit for those seeking a genuine Fado experience.

- Address: Beco do Espírito Santo 1, 1100-222 Lisbon
- Phone: +351 21 886 8209
- Website: https://www.parreirinhadealfama.com/

Wine Bars

1. Black Sheep

Located in the heart of Lisbon, Black Sheep is a wine bar and shop that stands out for its carefully selected wines, cheeses, and charcuterie from artisanal producers. The knowledgeable staff provides insights into their curated wine list, enhancing the tasting experience.

- Address: Rua dos Douradores 205, 1100-207 Lisbon
- Phone: +351 21 886 2491
- Website: https://www.blacksheep.pt/

2. BA Wine Bar do Bairro Alto

This intimate wine bar offers an extensive selection of Portuguese wines, complemented by a variety of cheeses and charcuterie. The knowledgeable staff guides guests through the wine list, ensuring a personalized experience.

- Address: Rua da Rosa 107, 1200-382 Lisbon
- Phone: +351 21 346 1182
- Website: https://www.bawinebar.pt/

3. Comida Independente

Bridging the gap between shop, restaurant, and wine bar, Comida Independente emphasizes small-brand, regional wines from Portugal and beyond. The shelves are loaded with interesting and delicious selections, making it a favorite among wine professionals and enthusiasts.

- Address: Rua Cais das Naus Lote 2.21.01, 1990-173 Lisbon
- Phone: +351 21 152 5380
- Website: https://www.comidaindependente.pt/

Best Markets: Time Out Market & Mercado de Campo de Ourique

Lisbon's culinary landscape is a vibrant tapestry woven with traditional flavors and contemporary innovations. Central to this scene are its bustling markets, where locals and visitors converge to savor the city's gastronomic delights. Two standout destinations in this regard are the Time Out Market and the Mercado de Campo de Ourique. This chapter delves into the unique offerings of these markets, providing essential details such as addresses, contact information, and websites to enhance your culinary exploration of Lisbon.

Time Out Market

Address: Mercado da Ribeira, Avenida 24 de Julho, 1200-479 Lisboa, Portugal

Contact: +351 210 607 403 | infolisboa@timeoutmarket.com

Website: https://www.timeoutmarket.com/lisboa/

Overview:

Established in 2014 within the historic Mercado da Ribeira, the Time Out Market has swiftly become a culinary landmark in Lisbon. This innovative food hall concept brings together some of the city's top chefs, eateries, and cultural experiences under one roof, offering visitors a curated taste of Lisbon's best.

Culinary Highlights:

- Variety of Cuisine: The market boasts over 20 restaurants, 8 bars, and numerous shops, each selected by Time Out's editorial team to represent the pinnacle of Lisbon's food scene. From traditional Portuguese dishes to international fare, there's something to satisfy every palate.

- Renowned Chefs: Esteemed chefs like Henrique Sá Pessoa and Marlene Vieira have establishments within the market, allowing visitors to sample high-quality cuisine in a casual setting.

- Fresh Produce: In addition to prepared foods, the market retains its traditional roots by offering fresh produce, meats, and seafood, reflecting its origins as a central marketplace.

Operating Hours:

Open daily from 10:00 AM to 12:00 AM, providing flexibility for both lunch and dinner plans.

Getting There:

Conveniently located near the Cais do Sodré station, the market is easily accessible via public transportation, including trains, trams, and buses.

Mercado de Campo de Ourique

Address: Rua Coelho da Rocha 104, 1350-075 Lisboa, Portugal

Contact: +351 218 172 063

Website: https://www.mercadodecampodeourique.pt/

Overview:

Since its establishment in 1934, the Mercado de Campo de Ourique has been a cornerstone of the Campo de Ourique neighborhood. In 2013, the market underwent a significant renovation, transforming it into a modern food hall while preserving its traditional charm. Today, it serves as a beloved gathering spot for locals and a hidden gem for visitors seeking an authentic Lisbon experience.

Culinary Highlights:

- Diverse Food Stalls: The market features a variety of food stalls offering both traditional Portuguese dishes and international cuisine. From fresh seafood and artisanal cheeses to sushi and gourmet burgers, the options are diverse and enticing.

- Fresh Produce: True to its origins, the market continues to operate as a traditional market during the day, offering fresh fruits, vegetables, meats, and fish to shoppers.

- Community Atmosphere: With its cozy seating areas and communal tables, the market fosters a warm and inviting atmosphere, making it an ideal place to mingle with locals and enjoy leisurely meals.

Operating Hours:

- Sunday to Wednesday: 10:00 AM to 11:00 PM

- Thursday to Saturday: 10:00 AM to 1:00 AM

Note: Some fresh produce stalls may close earlier in the day.

Getting There:

Accessible via tram 28, alighting at the final stop, Campo de Ourique. The market is also reachable by various bus lines and is a pleasant walk from nearby neighborhoods.

Chapter 6

Sunset Cruises on the Tagus River

Lisbon is a city of breathtaking views, rich history, and unparalleled charm, but few experiences can compare to watching the sun set over the Tagus River from the deck of a boat. A sunset cruise on the Tagus River offers a magical way to see Lisbon from a unique perspective, taking in its famous landmarks bathed in golden hues while enjoying a relaxing and romantic atmosphere. Whether you're looking for a luxurious sailing adventure, a casual boat tour with live music, or a private yacht experience, there's a perfect cruise for every traveler.

In this chapter, we will explore what makes a sunset cruise in Lisbon so special, the best types of cruises available, what to expect, and how to choose the right one for your itinerary.

Why Take a Sunset Cruise in Lisbon?
1. Spectacular Views of Lisbon's Landmarks

A boat tour along the Tagus River provides a front-row seat to some of Lisbon's most iconic landmarks. As you sail along the river, you will see:

Belém Tower – A 16th-century fortress and UNESCO World Heritage Site.

Padrão dos Descobrimentos – The Monument to the Discoveries, honoring Portugal's great explorers.

Cristo Rei Statue – Lisbon's version of Rio's Christ the Redeemer, offering stunning views from the opposite side of the river.

25 de Abril Bridge – Often compared to San Francisco's Golden Gate Bridge, this suspension bridge is a breathtaking sight at sunset.

Praça do Comércio – The grand riverside square with its yellow buildings and the iconic Rua Augusta Arch.

2. The Romance and Relaxation of the River

Lisbon is known for its romantic atmosphere, and there are few things more enchanting than watching the sun dip below the horizon while drifting along the Tagus. The city lights begin to twinkle as night falls, creating a picturesque scene perfect for couples, photographers, and anyone who loves a peaceful, scenic experience.

3. A Unique Perspective of Lisbon

While Lisbon's viewpoints (miradouros) offer stunning cityscapes, a boat cruise provides an entirely different perspective. From the water, you can admire the city's hills, historic buildings, and bridges in a way that you simply can't from land.

4. Perfect for Any Type of Traveler

Whether you're visiting Lisbon solo, as a couple, with friends, or as a family, a sunset cruise caters to all types of travelers. Many cruises offer additional amenities such as wine tastings, live music, or private charters, allowing you to tailor the experience to your preferences.

Types of Sunset Cruises on the Tagus River

1. Traditional Sailboat Cruises

For a classic maritime experience, traditional sailboat cruises provide an authentic way to explore the Tagus. These wooden boats offer a more intimate setting and often include a small group of passengers, making them ideal for a romantic evening or a quiet retreat.

What to Expect:

A peaceful, wind-powered journey along the river.

Stunning sunset views without engine noise.

Complimentary drinks, such as Portuguese wine or a glass of sparkling vinho verde.

Best For: Couples, photographers, and those seeking a tranquil experience.

2. Catamaran Sunset Tours

Catamarans offer a larger and more stable cruising experience, making them perfect for groups, families, or travelers looking for a social atmosphere. Many catamaran tours feature live music, a bar, and comfortable lounging areas.

What to Expect:

Spacious decks with seating for relaxation.

The opportunity to mingle with other travelers.

Drinks and snacks available onboard.

Best For: Groups, families, and travelers who enjoy a lively atmosphere.

3. Luxury Yacht Charters

For those looking for a VIP experience, private yacht charters are an excellent choice. These high-end cruises offer exclusive services, gourmet dining, and customized itineraries.

What to Expect:

Personalized service, often with a private skipper.

The option to bring your own playlist and enjoy a private setting.

High-quality meals or wine tastings onboard.

Best For: Honeymooners, special occasions, and luxury travelers.

4. Budget-Friendly Group Cruises

If you're traveling on a budget but still want to enjoy the beauty of Lisbon from the water, many affordable group tours offer sunset cruises at reasonable prices.

What to Expect:

Larger boats accommodating more passengers.

A lively atmosphere with music and drinks.

Great value for money.

Best For: Budget travelers, backpackers, and solo travelers looking to meet others.

5. Themed Cruises (Live Music, Fado, or Wine Tastings)

For a unique touch, some cruises incorporate live Fado performances, jazz music, or guided wine tastings. These cruises blend entertainment with sightseeing, offering an unforgettable evening on the river.

- What to Expect:
    - o A blend of sightseeing and cultural experiences.
    - o Wine, cocktails, or gourmet food options.
    - o A memorable night with a distinctly Portuguese atmosphere.
- Best For: Music lovers, foodies, and travelers seeking a cultural experience.

What to Expect on a Sunset Cruise

Duration

Most sunset cruises last between 1.5 to 2 hours, allowing plenty of time to enjoy the river views and relax before heading back to shore.

Departure Points

Popular departure locations include:

- Doca de Santo Amaro (Near the 25 de Abril Bridge) – A common starting point for luxury yachts and catamarans.
- Belém Marina – A historical area close to major landmarks.
- Cais do Sodré – Central and convenient for those staying in downtown Lisbon.

Typical Inclusions

- Welcome drink (wine, beer, or a soft drink).
- Guided commentary about Lisbon's history and landmarks.
- Comfortable seating with outdoor and indoor options.

Optional Extras

Some cruises offer premium add-ons such as:

- Private dinner options onboard.
- Champagne upgrades for special occasions.
- Photographer services for professional sunset photos.

How to Choose the Right Sunset Cruise

Consider Your Budget

- Luxury yachts can cost over €100 per person.
- Catamaran or sailboat tours range from €30-€60 per person.
- Budget-friendly group cruises start at €20 per person.

Think About the Atmosphere

- Romantic sunset sailboats are perfect for couples.
- Lively catamaran tours suit social travelers.
- Private charters offer an exclusive, VIP experience.

Check the Departure Time

- Sunset times vary throughout the year, so check seasonal schedules.
- Arrive at least 15 minutes early to board smoothly.

Read Reviews and Book in Advance

- Popular cruises sell out quickly, especially in summer.
- Platforms like GetYourGuide, Viator, and Airbnb Experiences offer reliable bookings.

Exploring Lisbon's Street Art Scene

Lisbon's vibrant street art scene has transformed the city into an open-air gallery, where murals and installations narrate tales of its rich history, culture, and contemporary issues. This chapter delves into the heart of Lisbon's urban artistry, highlighting key locations, notable artworks, and essential details to guide your exploration.

1. Galeria de Arte Urbana (GAU)
Address: Calçada da Glória, 1250-096 Lisboa, Portugal

Overview:

Established in 2008, the Galeria de Arte Urbana (GAU) is a pioneering initiative by the Lisbon City Council aimed at promoting and legitimizing street art. Located along the steep Calçada da Glória, this open-air gallery features rotating murals by both local and international artists, making it a dynamic canvas that reflects the evolving urban art scene.

Highlights:

- Rotating Exhibitions: The walls of GAU are periodically refreshed, offering new artworks that keep the space lively and engaging.

- Artist Collaborations: GAU has hosted works by renowned artists, contributing to its reputation as a significant cultural landmark in Lisbon.

Visiting Tips:

- Accessibility: The site is easily accessible via the Elevador da Glória funicular, which connects Praça dos Restauradores to Bairro Alto.

- Best Time to Visit: Early mornings or late afternoons provide optimal lighting for photography and a quieter atmosphere for appreciation.

2. Amoreiras Wall of Fame
Address: Avenida Conselheiro Fernando de Sousa, 1070-051 Lisboa, Portugal

Overview:

The Amoreiras Wall of Fame is a prominent street art hotspot in Lisbon, featuring large-scale murals by both established and emerging artists. This expansive wall serves as a legal canvas, encouraging creativity and expression within the urban environment.

Highlights:

- Diverse Artworks: The wall showcases a variety of styles and themes, reflecting the diversity of Lisbon's street art community.

- Community Engagement: Regular events and live painting sessions foster interaction between artists and the public.

Visiting Tips:

- Accessibility: Located near the Amoreiras Shopping Center, the site is easily reachable by public transportation, including buses and the metro.

- Best Time to Visit: Weekends often feature live painting events, offering a chance to witness the creative process firsthand.

3. LX Factory
Address: Rua Rodrigues de Faria 103, 1300-501 Lisboa, Portugal

Contact: +351 213 144 398

Website: https://lxfactory.com/

Overview:

Once an industrial complex, LX Factory has been transformed into a creative hub housing shops, restaurants, and studios. The site's walls are adorned with vibrant murals and installations, making it a must-visit destination for street art enthusiasts.

Highlights:

- Iconic Murals: Notable works include large-scale pieces by artists such as Bordalo II, known for his trash animal series.

- Artistic Atmosphere: The fusion of historical architecture and contemporary art creates a unique environment that inspires creativity.

Visiting Tips:

- Accessibility: Easily accessible via tram 15E or buses that stop near the Alcântara-Mar station.

- Best Time to Visit: Evenings are particularly lively, with markets and events adding to the vibrant atmosphere.

4. Quinta do Mocho
Address: Rua Padre Joaquim Alves Correia, 2685-223 Sacavém, Portugal

Overview:

Quinta do Mocho, located in the suburb of Sacavém, is home to one of Europe's largest open-air galleries. The neighborhood features over 100 murals, transforming it into a vibrant canvas that tells stories of community and culture.

Highlights:

- Guided Tours: Local organizations offer guided tours, providing insights into the artworks and the history of the community.

- Community Transformation: The street art initiative has played a significant role in revitalizing the area, fostering pride among residents.

Visiting Tips:

- Accessibility: Reachable by taking the metro to Oriente station, followed by a short bus ride.

- Best Time to Visit: Daytime visits are recommended to fully appreciate the scale and details of the murals.

5. Calçada da Glória
Address: Calçada da Glória, 1250-001 Lisboa, Portugal

Overview:

Calçada da Glória is a steep street connecting Praça dos Restauradores to Bairro Alto. It is renowned for its vibrant street art, with walls serving as canvases for dynamic murals and graffiti.

Highlights:

- Dynamic Artworks: The murals along Calçada da Glória are frequently updated, offering fresh visual experiences with each visit.

- Artistic Hub: The area attracts both local and international artists, contributing to its diverse artistic landscape.

Visiting Tips:

- Accessibility: The Elevador da Glória funicular provides a convenient and scenic route to the top of the hill.

- Best Time to Visit: Early mornings offer a quieter environment for art appreciation and photography.

6. Amoreiras Wall of Fame
Address: Avenida Conselheiro Fernando de Sousa, 1070-051 Lisboa, Portugal

Overview:

The Amoreiras Wall of Fame is a prominent street art hotspot in Lisbon, featuring large-scale murals by both established and emerging artists. This expansive wall serves as a legal canvas, encouraging creativity and expression within the urban environment.

Highlights:

- Diverse Artworks: The wall showcases a variety of styles and themes, reflecting the diversity of Lisbon's street art community.

- Community Engagement: Regular events and live painting sessions foster interaction between artists and the public.

Visiting Tips:

- Accessibility: Located near the Amoreiras Shopping Center, the site is easily reachable by public transportation, including buses and the metro.

- Best Time to Visit: Weekends often feature live painting events, offering a chance to witness the creative process firsthand.

Wine Tasting & Portuguese Cuisine Workshops

Lisbon is not just a city of breathtaking landscapes, historic architecture, and vibrant neighborhoods—it is also a paradise for food and wine lovers. The Portuguese capital offers countless opportunities to explore its rich culinary heritage and renowned wines, with experiences ranging from intimate wine tastings to hands-on cooking workshops where visitors can learn the secrets of traditional Portuguese dishes.

Whether you are a casual enthusiast or a seasoned gourmand, Lisbon's food and wine experiences promise a deeper connection to the city's culture, traditions, and local flavors. This chapter explores the best wine-tasting spots and cooking classes in Lisbon, providing details on where to go, what to expect, and how to make the most of these experiences.

Wine Tasting in Lisbon

Portugal is one of the world's oldest wine-producing countries, with a history that dates back thousands of years. Lisbon, as a gateway to some of Portugal's most renowned wine regions—such as Douro Valley, Alentejo, and Setúbal—is a fantastic place to indulge in wine-tasting experiences.

Why Experience Wine Tasting in Lisbon?

- Portugal is home to unique grape varieties found nowhere else in the world, such as Touriga Nacional, Trincadeira, and Baga.
- Portuguese wine regions have diverse climates, creating a wide range of flavors, from bold reds to crisp whites and refreshing "green wines" (Vinho Verde).
- Lisbon is close to Setúbal and Alentejo, two wine-producing regions known for their rich reds, fortified Moscatel wines, and excellent aging potential.

Best Wine Tasting Experiences in Lisbon

1. Lisbon Winery
Address: Rua da Barroca 13, 1200-047 Lisboa
Contact: +351 966 543 080
Website: www.lisbonwinery.com

Lisbon Winery is one of the city's best-kept secrets for wine lovers. This cozy wine bar and tasting room in the Bairro Alto district offers a selection of top Portuguese wines from across the country. Guests can enjoy expert-led tastings paired with artisanal cheeses, cured meats, and traditional petiscos (Portuguese tapas).

What to Expect:

- Intimate guided tastings led by knowledgeable sommeliers.
- Wine flights featuring a variety of reds, whites, and fortified wines.
- Perfect for both beginners and experienced wine drinkers.

Address: Rua das Flores 41, 1200-193 Lisboa
Contact: +351 213 420 319
Website: www.bythewine.pt

Owned by José Maria da Fonseca, one of Portugal's most historic wine producers, By The Wine is an elegant wine bar offering tastings of Setúbal Peninsula wines, including the famous Moscatel de Setúbal, a sweet fortified wine.

What to Expect:

- A stylish wine bar with walls lined with stacked wine bottles.
- Wine and food pairings, including charcuterie, seafood, and traditional Portuguese dishes.
- A laid-back yet sophisticated atmosphere in Lisbon's Chiado district.

2. Sommelier Lisbon Wine Bar
Address: Rua do Telhal 59, 1150-345 Lisboa
Contact: +351 968 658 651
Website: www.sommelierlisbon.com

Sommelier Lisbon is a wine lover's paradise with over 80 wines available by the glass. Each tasting is carefully curated, offering a deep dive into Portugal's winemaking traditions.

What to Expect:

- Customized tastings based on personal preferences.
- A selection of Portuguese wines from all regions, including Vinho Verde, Douro, and Alentejo.
- Expert sommeliers who guide you through each wine's history, region, and pairing options.

Portuguese Cuisine Workshops in Lisbon
One of the best ways to connect with Lisbon's food culture is by taking part in a cooking class. Whether learning how to make the famous Pastéis de Nata (custard tarts) or a hearty

seafood cataplana, Lisbon offers a variety of workshops where visitors can master the art of Portuguese cuisine.

Why Take a Cooking Class in Lisbon?

- Hands-on experience with fresh, locally sourced ingredients.
- Learn from local chefs who share family recipes and culinary secrets.
- Enjoy a delicious meal that you cooked yourself, often accompanied by Portuguese wines.

Best Cooking Workshops in Lisbon

1. Cooking Lisbon
Address: Rua Bernardim Ribeiro 9, 1150-071 Lisboa
Contact: +351 916 047 883
Website: www.cookinglisbon.com

Cooking Lisbon is one of the most popular cooking schools in the city, offering traditional Portuguese cooking classes in a friendly and relaxed environment.

What to Expect:

- A hands-on experience, preparing a 3-course meal with guidance from a professional chef.
- Dishes include Bacalhau à Brás (salted cod with eggs and potatoes), Caldo Verde (Portuguese green soup), and Pastéis de Nata.
- Wine pairing included with the meal.

2. Pastel de Nata Workshop at Manteigaria
Address: Rua do Loreto 2, 1200-108 Lisboa
Contact: +351 213 471 492
Website: www.manteigaria.com

Manteigaria, one of Lisbon's most famous bakeries, offers workshops where visitors can learn how to make their own Pastéis de Nata, Portugal's signature custard tart.

What to Expect:

- Learn how to make the perfect flaky pastry and creamy custard filling.
- A behind-the-scenes experience in one of Lisbon's top pastry shops.
- Take-home recipe so you can recreate the tarts at home.

Beaches Near Lisbon: Costa da Caparica & Guincho

Lisbon, with its unique blend of history, culture, and vibrant urban life, also offers easy access to some of Portugal's most stunning beaches. Within a short distance from the city center, you can find a variety of coastal retreats, from long stretches of golden sand to rugged, dramatic shorelines. Among the best-known and most popular beaches near Lisbon are Costa da Caparica and Praia do Guincho. These two beach destinations cater to different preferences—whether you seek a laid-back sunbathing spot or an adventurous surfing paradise.

Costa da Caparica: A Beach Lover's Paradise
Overview

Costa da Caparica is a 15-kilometer-long stretch of sandy coastline located just 15 km south of Lisbon. It is one of the most accessible beach areas from the capital and a favorite among locals and tourists alike. The coastline is divided into various beaches, some more developed with beach bars and restaurants, while others remain untouched and tranquil.

Why Visit Costa da Caparica?

- Golden Sand and Clear Waters – The beaches here offer soft golden sand and Atlantic waves that vary from calm to medium intensity, making it suitable for both relaxation and water sports.
- Easy Accessibility – Just a 30-minute drive or a short bus ride from Lisbon, this area is convenient for a day trip.
- Beachfront Restaurants and Bars – Enjoy fresh seafood and cocktails while gazing at the ocean.
- Surfing and Water Sports – With consistent waves, Costa da Caparica is a hotspot for surfing, bodyboarding, and kitesurfing.
- Laid-Back Atmosphere – Compared to the more commercialized Algarve beaches, Costa da Caparica retains a relaxed and welcoming vibe.

Best Beaches in Costa da Caparica

Costa da Caparica is not just one beach but a collection of smaller beaches along the coast. Here are some highlights:

1. Praia da Princesa
Why go? This beach is known for its trendy bars and lively atmosphere. It's perfect for travelers looking to enjoy drinks, music, and a vibrant crowd.

2. Praia da Mata
Why go? If you prefer a quieter escape, Praia da Mata offers soft sand and fewer crowds, making it ideal for sunbathing and peaceful walks.

3. Fonte da Telha
Why go? This beach is further down the coast and is known for its more rugged, natural scenery. It attracts surfers and nature lovers alike.

How to Get to Costa da Caparica

- By Car: Drive across the 25 de Abril Bridge and follow signs to Costa da Caparica. The journey takes around 30 minutes.
- By Bus: Take bus 161 from Lisbon's Praça de Espanha, which takes about 40 minutes.
- By Ferry & Bus: Take a ferry from Cais do Sodré to Cacilhas, then hop on a bus to Costa da Caparica.

Praia do Guincho: A Wild and Windy Paradise

Overview

Located 35 km west of Lisbon, Praia do Guincho is one of Portugal's most breathtaking and dramatic beaches. Unlike the gentle, tourist-friendly beaches of Costa da Caparica, Guincho is known for its powerful waves, strong winds, and stunning natural scenery. It sits within the Sintra-Cascais Natural Park, surrounded by dunes and rugged cliffs.

Why Visit Praia do Guincho?

- Spectacular Natural Beauty – Golden dunes, dramatic cliffs, and vast ocean views make Guincho one of the most scenic beaches in Portugal.
- A Paradise for Surfers & Windsurfers – The strong winds and high waves make this a top destination for water sports enthusiasts.
- Proximity to Cascais & Sintra – A short drive from the charming town of Cascais and the historic Sintra, making it a perfect stop on a day trip.

- Less Crowded Than Other Beaches – Due to its wilder conditions, Guincho is less packed with tourists, allowing for a more serene experience.

Best Activities at Guincho Beach

1. Surfing & Windsurfing

Guincho Beach is one of the best surfing spots in Portugal. The strong Atlantic winds create excellent waves, drawing surfers from all over the world. Beginners can take lessons from local surf schools, while advanced surfers can enjoy the challenging conditions.

2. Hiking & Scenic Walks

Surrounded by the Sintra-Cascais Natural Park, Guincho offers stunning coastal trails. A walk along the cliffs provides breathtaking views of the Atlantic Ocean, making it a must for nature lovers and photographers.

3. Cycling from Cascais to Guincho

A bike path runs from Cascais to Guincho, offering a scenic 9 km ride along the coastline. You can rent bikes in Cascais and enjoy a leisurely cycle with sea views all the way to Guincho.

4. Watching the Sunset

The open Atlantic horizon makes Guincho one of the best places near Lisbon to watch the sunset. As the sun dips below the ocean, the sky turns a mixture of deep orange and purple—a truly unforgettable sight.

How to Get to Praia do Guincho

- By Car: Drive from Lisbon to Cascais, then follow the signs to Guincho. The trip takes about 40 minutes.
- By Train & Bus: Take a train from Cais do Sodré to Cascais, then catch bus 405 or 415 to Guincho Beach.

Which Beach Should You Choose?
Both Costa da Caparica and Praia do Guincho offer fantastic beach experiences, but the best choice depends on what kind of day at the beach you are looking for:

Beach	Best For	Atmosphere	Accessibility	Surfing?
Costa da Caparica	Families, sunbathers, casual beachgoers	Relaxed, social, fun beach bars	Easy – short drive or bus ride from Lisbon	Yes, but more beginner-friendly
Praia do Guincho	Adventure seekers, surfers, nature lovers	Wild, rugged, windy, less crowded	Slightly more remote – best reached by car	Yes, excellent for experienced surfers

Lisbon Nightlife: Rooftop Bars & Clubs

Lisbon is a city that comes alive at night, offering a vibrant nightlife scene that caters to all tastes. Whether you're looking for a relaxed evening with cocktails and panoramic city views or a night of dancing until sunrise, Lisbon has something for everyone. The city's rooftop bars and clubs are among the best places to experience its dynamic nightlife, offering breathtaking views, world-class DJs, and an unforgettable atmosphere.

This chapter explores the best rooftop bars for a stylish and scenic night out, followed by the top clubs where you can dance the night away.

Rooftop Bars in Lisbon
Lisbon's rooftops offer some of the best spots to enjoy a drink under the stars, with stunning views of the Tagus River, historic landmarks, and vibrant city lights. Here are some of the top rooftop bars in the city:

1. PARK Bar

Address: Calçada do Combro 58, Bairro Alto, 1200-115 Lisboa, Portugal
Opening Hours: Daily, 13:00 – 02:00
Website: https://www.instagram.com/park_bar_lisboa/

Why Visit?
PARK is one of Lisbon's most iconic rooftop bars, located on the top of a parking garage in Bairro Alto. With a laid-back vibe, wooden deck seating, and plenty of greenery, it feels like a hidden urban oasis.

Highlights:

- Panoramic views over Lisbon, including the 25 de Abril Bridge and Tagus River
- Relaxed ambiance during the day, transforming into a lively party spot at night
- Signature cocktails & local wines paired with delicious snacks and burgers
- Live DJs playing house, hip-hop, and chill-out music

Pro Tip: Arrive before sunset to grab a good spot and enjoy the golden hour over Lisbon.

2. Sky Bar Lisboa by SEEN

Address: Avenida da Liberdade 185, 1269-050 Lisboa, Portugal
Opening Hours: Daily, 17:00 – 01:00
Website: https://www.skybarrooftop.com/lisboa/

Why Visit?
Situated atop the Tivoli Avenida Liberdade Hotel, Sky Bar is a stylish and sophisticated rooftop bar with one of the best panoramic views in Lisbon.

Highlights:

- Luxurious atmosphere with plush seating and elegant decor
- Cocktail menu designed by expert mixologists
- Breathtaking views of Lisbon's skyline and the São Jorge Castle
- Live DJs and themed nights for a glamorous night out

Pro Tip: Dress smart-casual, as the venue has a chic dress code.

3. Topo Martim Moniz

Address: Centro Comercial Martim Moniz, Praça Martim Moniz 1100-341 Lisboa, Portugal
Opening Hours: Monday – Sunday, 12:00 – 00:00
Website: https://www.topo-lisboa.pt/

Why Visit?
Located in the multicultural Martim Moniz area, Topo is a trendy rooftop bar offering a stunning view of São Jorge Castle and the old town of Lisbon.

Highlights:

- Creative cocktails & craft beers
- Outdoor terrace with a relaxed atmosphere
- Fusion cuisine with Portuguese and international influences
- Affordable drinks compared to other rooftop bars

Pro Tip: Try their signature Lisbon Sunset cocktail, a mix of gin, citrus, and local ingredients.

4. Rio Maravilha

Address: LX Factory, Rua Rodrigues de Faria 103, 1300-501 Lisboa, Portugal
Opening Hours: Tuesday – Sunday, 12:30 – 00:00
Website: https://www.lxfactory.com/

Why Visit?
Located inside the LX Factory, Rio Maravilha is a creative

rooftop space inspired by Lisbon and Rio de Janeiro, offering a funky ambiance with artistic decor.

Highlights:

- Amazing view of the 25 de Abril Bridge
- Eclectic music selection with live performances
- Cocktail menu featuring Brazilian and Portuguese flavors
- Trendy, artsy decor with colorful murals and neon lights

Pro Tip: Visit during sunset for the best lighting and atmosphere.

Best Clubs in Lisbon
For those looking to dance the night away, Lisbon's clubs offer an eclectic mix of music, from electronic and house to Latin beats and hip-hop. Here are some of the best clubs in Lisbon:

1. Lux Frágil

Address: Avenida Infante Dom Henrique, 1950-376 Lisboa, Portugal
Opening Hours: Wednesday – Saturday, 23:00 – 06:00
Website: https://www.luxfragil.com/

Why Visit?
Regarded as Lisbon's best nightclub, Lux Frágil is a three-floor venue known for its world-class DJs, stylish decor, and electric atmosphere.

Highlights:

- Top international DJs and underground electronic music
- Multiple dance floors with different music styles
- Rooftop terrace overlooking the Tagus River

- Exclusive VIP section and stylish crowd

Pro Tip: Arrive early, as the club has strict entry policies and long queues.

2. MusicBox

Address: Rua Nova do Carvalho 24, 1200-161 Lisboa, Portugal
Opening Hours: Tuesday – Saturday, 23:00 – 06:00
Website: https://www.musicboxlisboa.com/

Why Visit?
Located in the Cais do Sodré district, MusicBox is a vibrant club and live music venue hosting independent bands, DJs, and experimental music.

Highlights:

- Underground and alternative music scene
- Live concerts and DJ sets
- Industrial-chic decor with a tunnel-like atmosphere

Pro Tip: This club is a great spot to discover emerging Portuguese artists.

3. Lust in Rio

Address: Cais da Viscondessa, 1200-109 Lisboa, Portugal
Opening Hours: Thursday – Saturday, 23:00 – 06:00
Website: https://www.lustinrio.com/

Why Visit?
An open-air club in the heart of Lisbon, Lust in Rio is perfect

for those who love dancing under the stars in a tropical party atmosphere.

Highlights:

- Latin, hip-hop, and electronic music nights
- Spacious outdoor dance floor with palm trees and lights
- Great cocktails and bottle service

Pro Tip: Visit on Thursday for their famous reggaeton and Latin nights.

4. Kremlin

Address: Escadinhas da Praia 5, 1200-764 Lisboa, Portugal
Opening Hours: Friday – Saturday, 00:00 – 06:00

Why Visit?
One of Lisbon's oldest and most famous electronic music clubs, Kremlin has been a techno lover's paradise since the 1980s.

Highlights:

- Underground and industrial aesthetic
- Top electronic DJs from Portugal and beyond
- Dark, intimate atmosphere with neon lighting

Pro Tip: If you're a fan of deep house and techno, this is the place to be.

Chapter 7

Best Shopping Streets & Malls in Lisbon

Lisbon is a shopper's paradise, offering everything from luxury boutiques and international brands to traditional markets and artisanal shops. Whether you're looking for fashion, home décor, handmade crafts, or unique souvenirs, the city has charming shopping streets, bustling malls, and hidden gems waiting to be explored.

This chapter provides a comprehensive guide to the best shopping streets and malls in Lisbon, ensuring you know exactly where to go for an unforgettable retail experience.

Best Shopping Streets in Lisbon

Lisbon's streets are filled with local shops, international fashion brands, and historic boutiques. The following shopping streets are must-visits for those looking to explore the city's retail scene.

1. Avenida da Liberdade – The Luxury Shopping Boulevard
Why Visit?

Avenida da Liberdade is Lisbon's most prestigious shopping street, known for its luxury boutiques, elegant architecture, and high-end brands. Often compared to Paris's Champs-Élysées, this tree-lined avenue is perfect for those looking for designer fashion, fine jewelry, and upscale shopping.

What to Find:

- Luxury brands like Louis Vuitton, Gucci, Prada, and Cartier
- High-end Portuguese designers such as Carolina Herrera and Hugo Boss
- Elegant cafés and five-star hotels for a relaxing break between shopping

Pro Tip: Even if luxury shopping isn't on your agenda, Avenida da Liberdade is worth visiting for its charming atmosphere and stunning architecture.

2. Rua Augusta – The Heart of Lisbon's Shopping Scene
Why Visit?
Rua Augusta is one of Lisbon's busiest pedestrian streets, lined with international brands, local shops, and charming outdoor cafés. It stretches from Rossio Square to the majestic Arco da Rua Augusta, offering a vibrant shopping experience in the city center.

What to Find:

- Popular international brands like Zara, Mango, and H&M
- Portuguese souvenir shops selling ceramics, cork products, and azulejos (tiles)
- Street performers and open-air dining

Pro Tip: Don't forget to walk through the Arco da Rua Augusta, which offers breathtaking views over Praça do Comércio and the Tagus River.

3. Bairro Alto & Príncipe Real – The Trendy & Bohemian Districts
Why Visit?
For those looking for boutique fashion, unique concept stores, and artisanal shops, Bairro Alto and Príncipe Real are

the perfect shopping districts. These areas attract a younger, stylish crowd looking for vintage fashion, home décor, and quirky souvenirs.

What to Find:

- Independent Portuguese designers like Embaixada Lisboa, a shopping gallery housed in a historic palace
- Vintage clothing stores and concept fashion shops
- Handmade jewelry, local cosmetics, and home décor

Pro Tip: Visit on a Saturday morning when Príncipe Real hosts the organic farmers' market, offering fresh produce, cheeses, and artisanal goods.

4. Chiado – The Elegant & Cultural Shopping District
Why Visit?
Chiado is Lisbon's most elegant shopping district, blending historic charm with modern sophistication. This area is home to century-old bookstores, stylish boutiques, and international brands, making it one of the most popular shopping areas in the city.

What to Find:

- Armazéns do Chiado, a small shopping center with popular brands
- Luxury Portuguese brands like Claus Porto (famous for handmade soaps)
- Historic bookstores, including Livraria Bertrand, the world's oldest bookstore

Pro Tip: Stop by Café A Brasileira, one of Lisbon's oldest cafés, for a traditional espresso and pastéis de nata while you shop.

175

Best Shopping Malls in Lisbon
For those who prefer an indoor shopping experience, Lisbon is home to modern malls with a mix of international brands, dining options, and entertainment.

1. Colombo Shopping Center – The Largest Mall in Lisbon
Address: Av. Lusíada 1500-392 Lisboa, Portugal
Opening Hours: Monday – Sunday, 08:00 – 00:00
Website: https://www.colombo.pt/

Why Visit?
Colombo is Lisbon's largest shopping mall, housing over 340 stores, a cinema, a food court, and even a bowling alley. It's the best place for fashion lovers, tech shoppers, and families looking for a day of shopping and entertainment.

What to Find:

- International brands like Zara, Nike, and Apple
- Portuguese retailers like Parfois and Bimba y Lola
- Cinema, arcade, and family-friendly entertainment options

Pro Tip: Take the Metro (Colégio Militar station) for easy access.

2. Amoreiras Shopping Center – The Stylish & Upscale Mall
Address: Av. Eng. Duarte Pacheco 1070-103 Lisboa, Portugal
Opening Hours: Monday – Sunday, 10:00 – 23:00
Website: https://www.amoreiras.com/

Why Visit?
Amoreiras is one of Lisbon's oldest and most stylish shopping centers, featuring a mix of luxury boutiques, designer brands, and gourmet stores.

What to Find:

- High-end fashion brands like Lacoste, Burberry, and Boss
- Portuguese brands and artisanal products
- Food court and gourmet supermarket for a fine dining experience

Pro Tip: Visit the Amoreiras 360° Panoramic View on the rooftop for a spectacular view of Lisbon.

3. Armazéns do Chiado – The Historic & Compact Mall
Address: Rua do Carmo 2, 1200-094 Lisboa, Portugal
Opening Hours: Monday – Sunday, 10:00 – 22:00
Website: https://www.armazensdochiado.com/

Why Visit?
Located in the heart of Chiado, this mall blends history and modern shopping in a beautifully restored 19th-century building.

What to Find:

- Fashion retailers like Fnac, Sephora, and Massimo Dutti
- A charming bookstore and specialty food shops
- Cafés and rooftop dining with scenic views

Pro Tip: This mall is perfect for quick shopping while exploring the cultural attractions in Chiado.

4. Vasco da Gama Shopping Center – The Modern Riverside Mall
Address: Av. Dom João II 1990-094 Lisboa, Portugal
Opening Hours: Monday – Sunday, 09:00 – 00:00
Website: https://www.centrovascodagama.pt/

Why Visit?
Located in the Parque das Nações district, Vasco da Gama Shopping Center is a modern mall with a scenic riverside setting, offering a mix of shopping, dining, and entertainment.

What to Find:

- Popular brands like Stradivarius, Adidas, and Fnac
- Multiple restaurants with river views
- Nearby attractions like the Lisbon Oceanarium and Telecabine cable cars

Pro Tip: Take a walk along the Tagus River promenade after shopping for a relaxing break.

Unique Lisbon Souvenirs to Bring Home

Lisbon is a city that captivates visitors with its rich history, charming streets, and vibrant culture. One of the best ways to preserve memories of your trip is by bringing home unique souvenirs that reflect the spirit of the city. Whether you're looking for traditional handicrafts, gourmet delights, or artistic treasures, Lisbon offers a variety of options to suit every taste and budget.

This chapter explores some of the best and most authentic souvenirs to take home from Lisbon, from hand-painted tiles and artisanal ceramics to delicious Portuguese delicacies and locally crafted products.

1. Azulejos (Traditional Portuguese Tiles)

Azulejos are hand-painted ceramic tiles that have been a part of Portuguese architecture and design for centuries. These tiles are often seen on Lisbon's buildings, churches, and metro stations, featuring intricate patterns, floral designs, and historical scenes.

Where to Buy:

- Fábrica Sant'Anna – Rua do Alecrim 95, 1200-015 Lisboa (www.fabrica-santanna.com)
- Solar Antiques – Rua Dom Pedro V 70, 1250-094 Lisboa (www.solar.com.pt)
- Cortiço & Netos – Rua Maria Andrade 37D, 1170-216 Lisboa

Tip: Many places sell replica azulejos, but for an authentic piece, visit Fábrica Sant'Anna, which has been producing hand-painted tiles since 1741.

2. Portuguese Cork Products
Portugal is the world's largest producer of cork, and Lisbon is a great place to find sustainable cork souvenirs. These include cork handbags, wallets, hats, coasters, notebooks, and even shoes.

Where to Buy:

- Cork & Co. – Rua das Salgadeiras 10, 1200-396 Lisboa (www.corkandcompany.pt)
- Pelcor – Rua das Pedras Negras 28, 1100-404 Lisboa
- EcoCork – Rua Augusta 172, 1100-054 Lisboa

Tip: Cork products are lightweight, durable, and eco-friendly, making them an ideal souvenir for travelers.

3. Portuguese Ceramics & Pottery

Portugal has a long tradition of ceramic craftsmanship, and Lisbon offers a wide selection of colorful ceramic bowls, plates, and decorative pieces. Many items feature traditional blue-and-white designs, while others showcase modern artistic interpretations.

Where to Buy:

- A Loja da Cerâmica – Rua Capelo 16, 1200-224 Lisboa
- Cerâmicas na Linha – Mercado de Campo de Ourique, Rua Coelho da Rocha 104, 1350-075 Lisboa
- Vista Alegre Store – Largo do Chiado 20, 1200-108 Lisboa (www.vistaalegre.com)

Tip: If you're looking for premium porcelain, Vista Alegre is Portugal's most famous ceramics brand, founded in 1824.

4. Portuguese Wine & Port

Portugal is known for its exceptional wines, and bringing home a bottle (or two) is a must. Some of the best options include:

- Port Wine – A fortified wine from the Douro Valley, best enjoyed as a dessert wine.
- Vinho Verde – A refreshing, slightly sparkling green wine from northern Portugal.
- Alentejo Wines – Full-bodied red wines from the Alentejo region.

Where to Buy:

- Garrafeira Nacional – Rua de Santa Justa 18, 1100-485 Lisboa (www.garrafeiranacional.com)

- The Wine Cellar – Rua Nova da Trindade 20 C, 1200-303 Lisboa
- By the Wine (José Maria da Fonseca) – Rua das Flores 41, 1200-193 Lisboa

Tip: If you're unsure which wine to buy, visit a wine bar for a tasting session before making your purchase.

5. Pastéis de Nata (Portuguese Custard Tarts) & Gourmet Treats

Lisbon's most famous pastry, the pastel de nata, is a delicious custard tart with a crispy, caramelized top. While they are best enjoyed fresh, you can buy pre-packaged versions or baking kits to recreate them at home.

Other gourmet souvenirs include:

- Flor de Sal – High-quality sea salt from the Algarve region.
- Portuguese Sardines – Available in beautifully designed tins.
- Ginja (Cherry Liqueur) – A sweet liqueur traditionally served in a chocolate cup.

Where to Buy:

- Manteigaria (for Pastéis de Nata) – Rua do Loreto 2, 1200-242 Lisboa (www.manteigaria.com)
- Conserveira de Lisboa (for Sardines) – Rua dos Bacalhoeiros 34, 1100-071 Lisboa
- Ginjinha Espinheira (for Ginja Liqueur) – Largo de São Domingos 8, 1150-320 Lisboa

181

Tip: If you love pastéis de nata, Manteigaria is one of the best places to buy a fresh one, and they also sell ready-to-bake versions.

6. Portuguese Embroidery & Linens

Portuguese embroidery is known for its intricate patterns and delicate hand-stitched details. You can find beautifully crafted:

- Tablecloths and napkins
- Hand-embroidered handkerchiefs
- Traditional "Lover's Handkerchiefs" (Lenços dos Namorados)

Where to Buy:

- A Vida Portuguesa – Largo do Intendente Pina Manique 23, 1100-285 Lisboa (www.avidaportuguesa.com)
- Casa Macário – Rua Augusta 272, 1100-059 Lisboa
- Feira da Ladra Market – Campo de Santa Clara, 1100-471 Lisboa

Tip: The Lover's Handkerchiefs are a traditional romantic gift, originally embroidered by women for their loved ones.

7. Portuguese Leather Goods & Shoes

Portugal is known for its high-quality leather craftsmanship, particularly in shoes, handbags, and belts. Lisbon has several stores specializing in locally made leather products that are both stylish and durable.

Where to Buy:

- Luvaria Ulisses (for Leather Gloves) – Rua do Carmo 87-A, 1200-093 Lisboa
- Eureka Shoes – Rua Augusta 177, 1100-048 Lisboa (www.eurekashoes.com)
- Carlos Santos Shoes – Rua Garrett 77, 1200-203 Lisboa

Tip: If you want custom-made leather shoes, many Portuguese brands offer made-to-order services.

8. Portuguese Music & Fado CDs

Fado, Portugal's soulful traditional music, makes for a wonderful cultural souvenir. You can find CDs, vinyl records, or even handcrafted Portuguese guitars.

Where to Buy:

- Museu do Fado Gift Shop – Largo do Chafariz de Dentro 1, 1100-139 Lisboa
- FNAC Chiado – Armazéns do Chiado, Rua do Carmo 2, 1200-094 Lisboa
- Discoteca Amália – Rua da Assunção 37, 1100-044 Lisboa

Tip: Visit a live Fado performance in the Alfama district before buying a CD to experience authentic Fado music.

Where to Find Azulejos (Traditional Tiles) in Lisbon

Lisbon is a city of colors, and one of its most recognizable artistic elements is the azulejo—the stunning, hand-painted ceramic tiles that decorate everything from historic buildings and palaces to metro stations and modern art installations. These tiles have been a part of Portuguese culture for centuries, and they make for one of the most meaningful souvenirs you can bring home. Whether you're looking for antique azulejos with intricate Moorish designs, modern interpretations with a contemporary twist, or even a workshop to create your own, Lisbon offers a variety of places to find these artistic treasures.

In this chapter, we'll explore the best places to find authentic azulejos, from historic tile shops and artisan workshops to flea markets and museums.

The History of Azulejos in Portugal

Before diving into where to buy azulejos, it's worth understanding their historical and cultural significance. The word *azulejo* comes from the Arabic *al-zulaij*, meaning "polished stone," reflecting the Moorish influence that introduced these decorative tiles to Portugal in the 15th century. Over the centuries, Portuguese artisans adapted and refined the craft, creating the distinct blue-and-white designs that became a hallmark of the country's artistic identity.

Azulejos can be found throughout Lisbon, often depicting historical events, religious scenes, or geometric patterns. Today, they remain a beloved symbol of Portuguese heritage, making them a perfect souvenir for those looking to bring a piece of Lisbon's artistic charm home.

Best Places to Buy Azulejos in Lisbon

1. Fábrica Sant'Anna (Since 1741) – The Oldest Tile Factory in Lisbon

For those looking for traditional, handmade azulejos, Fábrica Sant'Anna is one of the most authentic places in Lisbon. This factory has been producing tiles by hand since 1741, using techniques that have remained unchanged for centuries.

Why Visit?

- Authentic handmade tiles, crafted using traditional techniques
- Factory tours to witness the tile-making process from start to finish
- Custom-made designs available for purchase

Address: Calçada da Boa-Hora 96, 1300-415 Lisboa, Portugal
Opening Hours: Monday – Friday, 10:00 AM – 7:00 PM
Website: https://www.santanna.com.pt/
Contact: +351 213 637 245

Pro Tip: If you're looking for high-quality reproductions of antique tiles, this is one of the best places to shop.

2. Solar Antiques – The Best Place for Antique Azulejos

Solar Antiques is one of the most famous shops in Lisbon for antique azulejos. If you're looking for genuine historical tiles from different centuries, this is the place to go.

Why Visit?

- Antique azulejos dating back to the 16th century
- Rare and unique pieces, many salvaged from historical buildings
- A true collector's paradise for authentic Portuguese tiles

Address: Rua Dom Pedro V 70, 1250-094 Lisboa, Portugal
Opening Hours: Monday – Friday, 10:00 AM – 7:00 PM |
Saturday, 11:00 AM – 1:00 PM

Website: https://www.solarantiguidades.com/
Contact: +351 213 462 315

Pro Tip: If you're looking for one-of-a-kind tiles with historical value, Solar Antiques is a must-visit.

3. Cortiço & Netos – A Hidden Gem for Vintage Tiles

Cortiço & Netos is a lesser-known but fantastic shop for vintage and surplus tiles. Unlike other stores, it specializes in unused azulejos from the 20th century, making it a great spot to find retro designs from the 1960s and 70s.

Why Visit?

- A wide selection of vintage azulejos
- Affordable prices compared to antique shops
- Perfect for those looking for colorful and bold mid-century tile designs

Address: Rua Maria Andrade 37D, 1170-216 Lisboa, Portugal
Opening Hours: Monday – Friday, 11:00 AM – 7:00 PM | Saturday, 10:00 AM – 1:00 PM
Website: https://www.corticoenetos.com/
Contact: +351 218 853 056

Pro Tip: If you love mid-century aesthetics, this shop offers some of the best selections in Lisbon.

4. Feira da Ladra – Lisbon's Famous Flea Market

Feira da Ladra is Lisbon's oldest and most famous flea market, where you can find a treasure trove of antique and vintage azulejos. Many vendors sell individual tiles, often at bargain prices.

Why Visit?

- Affordable options for travelers on a budget
- Unique and random finds, from historical tiles to modern reproductions
- Great place to buy mixed azulejos for a DIY home project

Address: Campo de Santa Clara, 1100-472 Lisboa, Portugal
Opening Hours: Tuesday & Saturday, 6:00 AM – 5:00 PM

Pro Tip: Arrive early to get the best selection, and don't be afraid to negotiate prices.

5. Museu Nacional do Azulejo – The Tile Museum Shop

If you want to learn about the history of azulejos before purchasing one, visit the Museu Nacional do Azulejo. The museum's gift shop sells hand-painted reproductions of historic tiles, making it an excellent place to buy museum-quality souvenirs.

Why Visit?

- Educational experience about the history of azulejos
- Museum-quality reproductions available for purchase
- A great place to support local artisans

Address: Rua da Madre de Deus 4, 1900-312 Lisboa, Portugal
Opening Hours: Tuesday – Sunday, 10:00 AM – 6:00 PM
Website: https://www.museudoazulejo.gov.pt/
Contact: +351 218 100 340

Pro Tip: The museum is located in a beautiful 16th-century convent, so take time to explore before heading to the shop.

Azulejo Workshops: Make Your Own Tile

If you want a truly unique souvenir, why not make your own azulejo? Several studios in Lisbon offer tile-painting workshops, where you can create a personalized piece of art.

Best Places for Azulejo Workshops:

- Fundação Ricardo do Espírito Santo Silva – Offers workshops in traditional tile painting
- Luzia's Azulejo Workshop – Run by a local artist, perfect for small groups
- Cerâmica São Vicente – Hands-on experience in a real ceramic studio

Chapter 8

How to Travel Lisbon on a Budget

Lisbon is one of Europe's most affordable capital cities, making it an excellent destination for budget travelers. With its rich history, stunning architecture, and vibrant culture,

Lisbon offers an unforgettable experience without requiring a lavish budget.

This guide will provide practical tips on how to save money while exploring Lisbon, covering accommodation, food, transportation, attractions, and other travel expenses. Whether you're a backpacker, a digital nomad, or simply trying to cut costs, these strategies will help you make the most of your Lisbon adventure without breaking the bank.

1. Finding Budget-Friendly Accommodation: Accommodation in Lisbon can range from luxury hotels to budget hostels and affordable Airbnb rentals. To keep costs low, consider the following options:

Budget-Friendly Neighborhoods to Stay In

- Alfama – One of the most charming historic districts with many budget guesthouses.
- Mouraria – A diverse and authentic neighborhood, great for experiencing local culture.
- Graça – Offers fantastic views and a quieter atmosphere, with more affordable options.
- Bairro Alto – Known for its nightlife, you can find cheap hostels here, but it may be noisy at night.

Types of Budget Accommodation

1. Hostels – A great option for solo travelers or groups. Many Lisbon hostels offer free breakfast and social activities.

    o Popular budget-friendly hostels:

        ▪ Home Lisbon Hostel (affordable and highly rated)

- We Love F. Tourists Hostel (great location)
2. Guesthouses & Pensions – Small, family-run accommodations that offer a cozy, affordable alternative to hotels.

3. Airbnb & Short-Term Rentals – If traveling in a group, renting an apartment can be cheaper than multiple hotel rooms.

4. Couchsurfing – A free way to meet locals and experience Lisbon authentically.

Money-Saving Tip: Book in advance, especially in peak seasons (spring and summer), to secure the best rates.

2. Saving Money on Transportation
Lisbon is a walkable city, but public transportation is necessary for reaching certain areas.

Public Transportation Options

- Lisbon Metro – The cheapest and most efficient way to travel. A single ticket costs €1.80, but a 24-hour pass (€6.80) covers unlimited metro, buses, and trams.
- Buses & Trams – A single ticket on board is €3.00, so using a prepaid card (like Viva Viagem) is more economical.
- Ferries – Traveling across the Tagus River is cheap (around €1.30-€2.75 per ride).
- Train to Sintra & Cascais – Instead of expensive tours, take the train for just €2.30-€4.60 each way.

Transportation Discounts

- Viva Viagem Card – A rechargeable card that offers significant savings compared to single-ride fares.
- Lisbon Card – A tourist pass that provides unlimited public transport and free/discounted entry to many attractions (starting at €22 for 24 hours).
- Walking & Biking – Lisbon is hilly, but many areas are pedestrian-friendly. Bike rentals are available from €3 per hour.

Money-Saving Tip: Avoid taxis and opt for public transportation or ride-sharing apps like Bolt, which is cheaper than Uber in Lisbon.

3. Eating on a Budget: Where & What to Eat Cheaply
Lisbon has a fantastic food scene, and you don't need to spend a fortune to enjoy it.

Where to Find Affordable Meals

- Tascas (local eateries) – These small, family-run restaurants serve cheap and traditional Portuguese meals.
- Cafés & Bakeries – Perfect for affordable breakfast or snacks. A coffee and pastry cost around €2-€3.
- Supermarkets & Local Markets – Buy fresh produce, bread, and cheese for budget-friendly meals.
- Time Out Market (Mercado da Ribeira) – Offers diverse food stalls; prices are higher but reasonable.

Budget-Friendly Food Options

1. Bifana – A pork sandwich that costs around €3 at local snack bars.
2. Sardinhas Assadas (grilled sardines) – Found in many restaurants for €5-€10.
3. Menu do Dia – Many restaurants offer a set lunch menu (starter, main, dessert, and drink) for €8-€12.

4. Pastéis de Nata – Lisbon's famous custard tarts cost around €1-€1.50 each.

Money-Saving Tip: Avoid tourist restaurants in places like Praça do Comércio or Belém—they charge premium prices.

4. Free & Cheap Attractions in Lisbon

Lisbon has plenty of attractions that are either free or low-cost.

Free Attractions & Activities

- Miradouros (Viewpoints) – Beautiful panoramic views at spots like Miradouro de Santa Catarina and Miradouro da Senhora do Monte.
- Walking Tours – Many companies offer free walking tours, where you tip what you can.
- Beaches – The beaches near Lisbon, like Carcavelos and Costa da Caparica, are free and accessible by public transport.
- Exploring Alfama – Wander through Lisbon's oldest district for free.

Cheap Attractions with Discounts

- Belém Tower – Free on the first Sunday of each month; otherwise, entry is €6.
- Jerónimos Monastery – Free on Sundays before 2 PM; regular entry €10.
- Castelo de São Jorge – Offers student and senior discounts; regular entry is €10.

Money-Saving Tip: Visit museums and historic sites on free entry days (usually the first Sunday of the month).

5. Budgeting for Nightlife & Entertainment

Lisbon's nightlife is lively but doesn't have to be expensive.

How to Enjoy Nightlife on a Budget

- Pre-drink at Kiosks – Many locals buy drinks from kiosks in public squares, where a beer costs around €2.
- Happy Hours – Many bars offer discounted cocktails and beer before 9 PM.
- Live Fado Music – Avoid tourist traps and head to Tasca do Chico, where Fado performances are free (but buying a drink is expected).
- Clubs with Free Entry – Some clubs, like Musicbox and Park Bar, offer free entry on certain nights.

6. Smart Shopping & Souvenirs on a Budget

Avoid overpriced souvenirs in tourist-heavy areas. Instead, check out:

- Feira da Ladra – A flea market with cheap, authentic items.
- A Vida Portuguesa – Unique Portuguese gifts at reasonable prices.
- Supermarkets – Buy local wines, olive oil, or canned sardines as affordable souvenirs.

Money-Saving Tip: Shop in local markets instead of tourist souvenir shops.

Free & Affordable Attractions in Lisbon

Lisbon is one of Europe's most exciting destinations, offering rich history, stunning architecture, and a vibrant cultural scene. While it is often considered an affordable city compared to other Western European capitals, costs can add up quickly. Fortunately, Lisbon has plenty of free and low-cost attractions that allow visitors to explore its beauty without breaking the bank.

From breathtaking viewpoints and historic neighborhoods to museums with free admission days, there are numerous ways to enjoy Lisbon on a budget. Whether you are wandering through its picturesque streets, taking in a live Fado performance, or soaking up the atmosphere at one of its many parks and plazas, Lisbon offers incredible experiences without the need for a hefty budget.

Explore the Historic Neighborhoods for Free

One of the best ways to discover Lisbon is by walking through its unique neighborhoods, each with its own charm and character.

Alfama – The Oldest and Most Picturesque Quarter

Alfama, Lisbon's oldest neighborhood, is a maze of narrow, winding streets filled with traditional houses, azulejo-covered buildings, and hidden courtyards. As you explore, you will find historical landmarks such as the Sé Cathedral and Miradouro de Santa Luzia, a scenic viewpoint that offers a breathtaking panorama of the city and the Tagus River.

Wandering through Alfama is like stepping back in time, and the best part is that you don't need to spend a cent to enjoy its charm. If you visit in June, you can experience the Festas de Santo António, a lively street festival with music, dancing, and grilled sardines.

Bairro Alto – A Neighborhood Full of Life

By day, Bairro Alto is a quiet and charming area filled with tiled buildings and small cafés. By night, it transforms into Lisbon's nightlife hub. Walking through this district and soaking in the atmosphere is completely free. Many bars have no cover charge, so you can enjoy live music and the vibrant social scene without spending much.

Baixa and Chiado – The Heart of Lisbon

Baixa is Lisbon's downtown area, home to grand squares, elegant boulevards, and architectural landmarks. Praça do Comércio, one of the city's most famous squares, is a fantastic place to admire the stunning riverfront views. Walking around Chiado, you will find historic bookstores, charming cafés, and street performers entertaining passersby.

Discover Lisbon's Stunning Viewpoints (Miradouros)
Lisbon is a city built on hills, which means it boasts an incredible number of miradouros (viewpoints) that provide spectacular views of the city and beyond. Most of these are completely free to visit.

Miradouro de Santa Catarina

This popular spot offers a relaxed atmosphere with stunning views of the Tagus River and the 25 de Abril Bridge. It's a great place to watch the sunset while listening to street musicians performing.

Miradouro da Senhora do Monte

Often considered the best viewpoint in Lisbon, this spot provides a breathtaking panoramic view of the city. It's less crowded than other miradouros, making it a peaceful place to take in the beauty of Lisbon.

Miradouro de São Pedro de Alcântara

Located in Bairro Alto, this viewpoint features a beautifully landscaped garden and a spectacular view of Lisbon's rooftops and São Jorge Castle. It's a great place to relax and take in the scenery.

Free Museum Days and Affordable Cultural Attractions
While Lisbon has many world-class museums, entrance fees can add up. Luckily, some museums offer free admission on specific days or have affordable ticket prices.

Free Museums on Sundays
Many of Lisbon's public museums and monuments offer free entry on Sundays before 2 PM for residents and visitors. These include:

- Museu Nacional do Azulejo (National Tile Museum) – Showcasing Portugal's famous azulejos (decorative tiles).
- Museu Nacional de Arte Antiga (National Museum of Ancient Art) – Home to an extensive collection of European and Portuguese art.
- Museu do Aljube – Resistência e Liberdade – A museum dedicated to Portugal's history of resistance against dictatorship.

Affordable Museums and Attractions
Some museums are very budget-friendly, with ticket prices under €5.

- Museu do Fado – Learn about the history of Portugal's famous Fado music for an entry fee of around €5.
- Museu do Oriente – A fascinating museum showcasing Portugal's connections with Asia, with free admission on Fridays after 6 PM.

- Lisbon Story Centre – A great way to understand Lisbon's history through interactive exhibits, with tickets under €10.

Enjoy Lisbon's Parks and Gardens

Lisbon has many beautiful parks and green spaces that offer a great way to relax and enjoy nature for free.

Jardim da Estrela

This lush park near the Estrela Basilica is perfect for a picnic, a walk, or simply relaxing. It features a small lake, sculptures, and a charming café.

Eduardo VII Park

Lisbon's largest park offers spectacular views of the city and the Tagus River from its highest point. The park's well-maintained gardens and tree-lined pathways make it a great place for a stroll.

Tapada das Necessidades

A lesser-known park with a romantic, wild charm. It's an ideal spot for escaping the busy city and enjoying a peaceful afternoon.

Free Cultural Experiences

Listen to Free Live Fado Music

Fado, Portugal's traditional soulful music, can be expensive in many restaurants. However, there are ways to experience it for free. Some bars and cafés in Alfama and Bairro Alto host free Fado nights. A Baiuca in Alfama and Tasca do Chico in Bairro Alto sometimes offer free Fado performances, though you may be expected to buy a drink.

Street Art and Public Art Installations

Lisbon has an incredible street art scene, with colorful murals and graffiti by renowned artists like Vhils and Bordalo II. Some of the best places to see street art for free include:

- LX Factory – A creative hub with impressive urban art.
- Avenida da Índia – An open-air gallery of large murals.
- Amoreiras Wall of Fame – A constantly evolving street art spot.

Use Public Transportation Smartly
While Lisbon's public transportation system is affordable, there are ways to save even more.

- Get a Viva Viagem Card – A reloadable card that offers discounted fares on trams, metro, buses, and ferries.
- Use the 24-Hour Public Transport Ticket – For €6.80, you can get unlimited travel for 24 hours, including the famous Tram 28.
- Walk Whenever Possible – Lisbon is a very walkable city, and exploring on foot allows you to discover hidden gems.

Affordable Day Trips from Lisbon
Day trips don't have to be expensive. Some of the best nearby destinations are accessible by public transport at low prices.

Sintra
A UNESCO World Heritage site filled with palaces, castles, and lush gardens. A round-trip train ticket from Lisbon's Rossio Station costs about €5.

Cascais
A charming coastal town with beautiful beaches and historic streets. A train ticket from Cais do Sodré station costs under €3 one way.

Costa da Caparica
A fantastic beach destination just across the Tagus River. You can reach it by bus or ferry for less than €5.

Here is the revised content without emojis:

Best Happy Hour Deals & Budget-Friendly Eats

Lisbon is one of Europe's most affordable capital cities, making it an excellent destination for travelers who want to enjoy a vibrant cultural experience without breaking the bank. Whether you're looking for wallet-friendly dining options, great happy hour deals, or ways to stretch your budget, Lisbon offers plenty of choices. From authentic local eateries and budget-friendly restaurants to affordable drinks and happy hour spots, this chapter covers the best ways to enjoy the city without overspending.

Why Lisbon is a Great Budget Destination

Lisbon remains one of the most cost-effective cities in Western Europe. The city is known for its affordable food, drinks, and attractions, making it possible to experience its charm even on a tight budget. While high-end restaurants and trendy bars exist, traditional eateries, local tascas (small Portuguese restaurants), and lively happy hour deals allow visitors to enjoy Lisbon's food and nightlife scene without spending too much.

General Budgeting Tips for Lisbon

- Eat Like a Local – Traditional Portuguese tascas and cafés offer delicious meals at lower prices compared to touristy restaurants.
- Drink House Wine & Local Beer – Portuguese wine is both affordable and high-quality. A glass of wine can cost as little as €2-€3, and local beer is even cheaper.
- Take Advantage of Happy Hour – Many bars and restaurants have discounted drinks and food specials in the early evening.
- Opt for Set Menus – Many local restaurants offer lunch menus (menu do dia) for €10 or less, which usually include a soup, main course, drink, and coffee.
- Try Food Markets – Instead of dining in expensive restaurants, visit local food markets, where you can sample a variety of dishes at reasonable prices.
- Shop at Pastelarias – Portuguese bakeries offer inexpensive yet delicious pastries, sandwiches, and coffee—perfect for a quick meal.
- Use Public Transport – A Viva Viagem card allows unlimited travel on trams, buses, and metros for just €6.60 per day, making it a cost-effective way to get around.

Best Budget-Friendly Eats in Lisbon
Lisbon's dining scene offers a wide range of affordable restaurants, tascas, and cafés where you can enjoy traditional Portuguese cuisine without spending too much.

1. Zé dos Cornos

Address: Beco dos Surradores 5, 1100-591 Lisboa
Average Price: €10-€15 per meal
Best for: Traditional Portuguese food in a no-frills setting

Zé dos Cornos is a hidden gem in downtown Lisbon that serves delicious grilled meats, homemade soups, and seafood dishes at affordable prices. The portions are generous, and the atmosphere is cozy. It is a great spot for trying bifana (pork sandwich), bacalhau (salt cod), and grilled sardines.

2. O Trevo

Address: Praça Luís de Camões 48, 1200-243 Lisboa
Average Price: €3-€7 per meal
Best for: Cheap but tasty bifanas

O Trevo is a classic Lisbon café famous for its bifana sandwiches—a simple yet flavorful snack made with thinly sliced marinated pork served on a fresh roll. Anthony Bourdain visited this spot and praised its authenticity and affordability. A bifana and a beer together cost less than €5.

3. A Merendinha do Arco

Address: Rua dos Sapateiros 230, 1100-581 Lisboa
Average Price: €8-€12 per meal
Best for: Home-cooked Portuguese meals

This traditional tasca is a local favorite for serving classic dishes like bacalhau à brás (salt cod with eggs and potatoes), grilled pork, and caldo verde (kale soup) at very reasonable prices. The setting is simple, but the food is authentic and flavorful.

4. Time Out Market (Mercado da Ribeira)

Address: Avenida 24 de Julho 49, 1200-479 Lisboa
Average Price: €7-€15 per dish

Best for: Trying multiple dishes from different chefs in one place

Time Out Market is one of Lisbon's most popular food markets, where you can sample affordable yet gourmet food from top chefs and local vendors. While some dishes can be on the pricier side, there are still budget-friendly options available, especially if you share plates with friends.

5. Casa da Índia

Address: Rua do Loreto 49, 1200-241 Lisboa
Average Price: €10-€15 per meal
Best for: Hearty Portuguese meals at low prices

Casa da Índia is a local institution known for its affordable and delicious Portuguese dishes. The grilled chicken, seafood rice, and codfish are all great choices, and the atmosphere is lively.

6. Café Beira Gare

Address: Praça Dom João da Câmara 4, 1200-027 Lisboa
Average Price: €5-€10 per meal
Best for: Quick and cheap traditional Portuguese snacks

Located near Rossio Station, this café serves some of the best bifanas in Lisbon for just a few euros. It is a great place to grab a cheap yet filling snack before exploring the city.

Best Happy Hour Deals in Lisbon
Lisbon has an exciting nightlife scene, and many bars offer happy hour specials that make drinking out more affordable. Here are some of the best places to enjoy discounted drinks and a fun atmosphere.

1. PARK Bar
Address: Calçada do Combro 58, 1200-115 Lisboa
Happy Hour: 5 PM - 8 PM
Best for: Rooftop views and cheap cocktails

PARK Bar is a rooftop bar with breathtaking views of Lisbon. During happy hour, you can enjoy discounted cocktails, wine, and beer while watching the sunset over the city.

2. A Tabacaria
Address: Rua Dom Pedro V 99, 1250-093 Lisboa
Happy Hour: 4 PM - 7 PM
Best for: Affordable beers and casual vibes

A Tabacaria is a laid-back bar in the trendy Príncipe Real neighborhood, offering cheap beers and cocktails during happy hour. It is a great spot to relax before heading out for the night.

3. O Bom O Mau e O Vilão
Address: Rua do Alecrim 21, 1200-292 Lisboa
Happy Hour: 6 PM - 9 PM
Best for: Cheap gin and tonics and a stylish atmosphere

This bar is known for its unique decor and great music. The happy hour deals include half-price gin and tonics, sangria, and craft beers.

4. Foxtrot
Address: Travessa de Santa Teresa 28, 1200-405 Lisboa
Happy Hour: 6 PM - 8 PM
Best for: Classic cocktails in a vintage setting

Foxtrot is one of Lisbon's best speakeasy-style bars, offering discounted classic cocktails like Negronis, Old Fashioneds, and Mojitos during happy hour.

Chapter 9

Secret Viewpoints & Lesser-Known Streets

Lisbon is a city of breathtaking vistas and charming, winding streets. While visitors flock to famous miradouros (viewpoints) like Miradouro de Santa Catarina or Miradouro da Senhora do Monte, there are several lesser-known spots that offer equally spectacular views without the crowds. Similarly, the city's backstreets, tucked-away alleys, and forgotten neighborhoods hold a treasure trove of history, culture, and hidden beauty. This chapter explores some of Lisbon's best-kept secrets for those looking to experience the city beyond the tourist hotspots.

Secret Viewpoints (Miradouros Escondidos)
Lisbon is known as the "City of Seven Hills," and that means plenty of panoramic views. While most tourists visit the well-known viewpoints, locals have their own quiet spots to admire the city's unique skyline. Here are some lesser-known miradouros worth visiting.

1. Miradouro da Penha de França
Location: Rua Marques da Silva, Penha de França
Tucked away in the residential neighborhood of Penha de França, this viewpoint offers an impressive panoramic view of Lisbon's rooftops stretching all the way to the Tagus River. Because it's off the usual tourist route, you'll find locals relaxing here, often enjoying a quiet sunset away from the bustling city center.

2. Miradouro do Monte Agudo

Location: Rua Heliodoro Salgado, Anjos
Perched between the neighborhoods of Anjos and Arroios, this hidden gem provides an expansive view of Lisbon's downtown area and beyond. With benches shaded by pine trees, it's an excellent spot for a peaceful afternoon break.

3. Miradouro do Largo das Necessidades
Location: Largo das Necessidades, Alcântara
This serene viewpoint sits next to the Palácio das Necessidades, a lesser-visited historical palace. Overlooking the Tagus River, this miradouro is particularly beautiful at sunset and is a perfect spot for a quiet moment of reflection.

4. Miradouro de Santo Amaro
Location: Near Capela de Santo Amaro, Alcântara
This tiny but stunning viewpoint is nestled within a small chapel courtyard, offering an amazing view of the Ponte 25 de Abril bridge and the Tagus River. It's rarely crowded, making it an ideal spot for photography.

5. Miradouro do Chão do Loureiro
Location: Rua do Chão do Loureiro, near Castelo de São Jorge
A hidden alternative to the busy viewpoints around the castle, this spot provides an incredible cityscape framed by the charm of a quiet residential area. It's also close to Elevador do Castelo, an elevator that connects the Baixa district to the castle area.

Lesser-Known Streets & Hidden Alleys
Lisbon's charm is not only found in its grand avenues and famous squares but also in its narrow, winding streets that hold stories of the past and a glimpse into everyday local life. Here are some of the most fascinating and lesser-known streets to explore.

1. Rua dos Remédios, Alfama
This narrow street in the heart of Alfama remains one of the most authentic places to experience old Lisbon. Lined with small fado houses, traditional taverns, and hidden artisan shops, Rua dos Remédios offers a nostalgic journey through Lisbon's oldest neighborhood. Walk down this street in the evening, and you'll hear the distant melodies of fado music drifting through the air.

2. Beco do Jasmim, Mouraria
A tiny alleyway in the Mouraria district, Beco do Jasmim is a beautiful escape from the crowded parts of the city. It is covered in colorful street art, with small cafés tucked into the corners. A perfect place for an afternoon coffee or to admire some of Lisbon's lesser-known artistic expressions.

3. Calçada do Duque, Baixa-Chiado
A charming stairway street that connects Restauradores Square to the upper part of the city near Bairro Alto, Calçada do Duque is lined with traditional Portuguese restaurants and offers one of the most picturesque walks in Lisbon. Fewer tourists venture here, making it an excellent spot for an evening stroll.

4. Rua da Bica de Duarte Belo
This street is often overshadowed by the famous Bica Funicular that runs through it. However, walking up or down this historic street at night, when the tram has stopped running, gives a completely different and peaceful experience. The old buildings, small bars, and traditional atmosphere make it one of Lisbon's most authentic streets.

5. Travessa do Cabral, Príncipe Real
This little-known alleyway in Príncipe Real leads to a hidden courtyard filled with lush greenery and charming cafés. It's a

wonderful place to take a break and enjoy a quiet moment away from the usual tourist spots.

6. Rua da Silva, Santos

Located in the creative and trendy district of Santos, Rua da Silva is filled with indie shops, hidden bookstores, and cozy bars. This area is perfect for those who love discovering local design and art.

Hidden Courtyards & Gardens

Beyond the viewpoints and streets, Lisbon also hides some lesser-known gardens and courtyards, perfect for those seeking quiet and relaxation.

1. Jardim do Torel

Location: Rua Júlio de Andrade

A peaceful green space with one of the best views over Avenida da Liberdade and downtown Lisbon. It's a great alternative to the busier parks and miradouros in the city.

2. Palácio Pombal Garden

Location: Rua de O Século 79, Bairro Alto

A hidden courtyard behind an 18th-century palace, this spot is home to lush plants, sculptures, and quiet seating areas, making it one of Lisbon's most relaxing hidden gems.

3. Jardim da Cerca da Graça

Location: Rua Damasceno Monteiro, Graça

This garden offers a beautiful retreat with open green spaces, fantastic city views, and a local feel. It's an ideal place for a picnic away from the usual crowds.

The Underrated Neighborhoods of Lisbon

Lisbon is famous for its historic landmarks, charming trams, and vibrant nightlife, but beyond the well-trodden paths of Alfama, Baixa, and Belém, there are lesser-known neighborhoods that offer an authentic and unique experience of the city. These underrated areas provide an alternative perspective of Lisbon, where local life thrives, hidden art flourishes, and historic charm meets contemporary creativity. For travelers looking to escape the crowds, these neighborhoods offer a deeper and more intimate connection with the city.

1. Campo de Ourique: The Perfect Blend of Tradition and Modernity

Campo de Ourique is often overlooked by tourists, yet it is one of Lisbon's most livable and charming neighborhoods. Situated west of Estrela, it is a peaceful yet lively district with a strong community feel, excellent food markets, and a rich cultural scene.

What Makes Campo de Ourique Special?

- Mercado de Campo de Ourique: A fantastic food market offering local delicacies and gourmet treats, often less crowded than Time Out Market.
- Casa Fernando Pessoa: The former home of Portugal's legendary poet Fernando Pessoa, now a museum and cultural center.
- Prazeres Cemetery: A hauntingly beautiful cemetery with stunning mausoleums and panoramic views of the Ponte 25 de Abril bridge.

- Cafés and Bakeries: Some of the best pastelarias in Lisbon, perfect for indulging in fresh pastéis de nata.

2. Graça: Authentic Lisbon with the Best Views

Graça sits on one of Lisbon's highest hills, offering incredible panoramic views of the city. While Alfama and Bairro Alto attract most visitors, Graça remains an undiscovered treasure for many.

Highlights of Graça

- Miradouro da Senhora do Monte: Arguably the best viewpoint in Lisbon, offering stunning sunsets and fewer crowds.
- Miradouro da Graça: Another breathtaking viewpoint, ideal for a drink with a view.
- Tile-Clad Streets and Old-World Charm: A neighborhood filled with traditional Portuguese architecture and beautiful azulejos.
- Tasca-Friendly Dining: Home to many hidden tascas serving authentic, homemade Portuguese cuisine at very affordable prices.

3. Alvalade: A Taste of Lisbon's Local Life

Alvalade is a residential neighborhood that has retained its mid-20th-century charm while embracing a modern, creative scene. It is ideal for travelers looking to experience Lisbon through the eyes of a local.

Why Visit Alvalade?

- Mercado de Alvalade Norte: A great place to sample fresh seafood, fruits, and local delicacies.

- Local Café Culture: Plenty of traditional cafés and bakeries where Lisboetas start their day.
- Street Art and Retro Vibes: A neighborhood that blends old-school architecture with colorful murals and trendy boutiques.

4. Alcântara: Industrial Cool Meets Riverside Relaxation

Alcântara is a neighborhood in transition, where old warehouses have been transformed into trendy spaces, and the riverside offers stunning walks and dining spots. It is home to the creative hub of LX Factory, but there is much more to explore beyond it.

What to Explore in Alcântara?

- LX Factory: A former industrial complex turned into a creative and cultural hotspot with shops, restaurants, and street art.
- Village Underground Lisboa: A unique cultural space made of repurposed buses and shipping containers, offering coworking, music, and events.
- Docas de Santo Amaro: A waterfront area with great seafood restaurants and bars overlooking the marina.

5. Penha de França: The Quiet Hilltop Retreat

Penha de França is one of Lisbon's least explored neighborhoods, despite its fantastic views and tranquil streets. It sits on a hill between Graça and Arroios and offers a peaceful alternative to the busier areas of the city.

Hidden Gems in Penha de França

- Jardim da Cerca da Graça: A peaceful park with beautiful views, perfect for a quiet afternoon.

- Local Cafés and Bakeries: Less touristy, offering some of the most affordable and delicious pastries.
- Street Art and Small Shops: The area has a growing artistic scene with colorful murals and unique local stores.

6. Ajuda: Lisbon's Forgotten Royal District

Ajuda is home to the often-overlooked Ajuda National Palace and offers a glimpse into Lisbon's regal past. It is a neighborhood filled with history, charm, and lesser-known gems.

What to See in Ajuda?

- Palácio Nacional da Ajuda: A stunning royal palace that is far less crowded than the famous Palácio da Pena in Sintra.
- Jardim Botânico da Ajuda: Lisbon's oldest botanical garden, a peaceful retreat filled with exotic plants.
- Pasteis de Belém Alternative: Instead of the famous (and often packed) Pastéis de Belém, try smaller pastry shops in Ajuda for an equally delicious but less crowded experience.

7. Marvila: Lisbon's Emerging Creative District

Marvila is an up-and-coming area, often compared to Berlin's Kreuzberg or London's Shoreditch. It is a mix of industrial warehouses, trendy breweries, and alternative art spaces.

What's Special about Marvila?

- Lisbon's Craft Beer Scene: Some of the best breweries, including Musa, Dois Corvos, and Lince.
- Underground Art Galleries: Unique spaces showcasing contemporary Portuguese art.
- Hidden Cafés and Restaurants: Creative eateries offering an experimental take on traditional dishes.

213

Local Experiences Beyond the Tourist Spots

Lisbon is one of Europe's most visited cities, but beyond the famous landmarks like Belém Tower, Tram 28, and the bustling streets of Baixa and Alfama, the city hides a wealth of lesser-known treasures. For travelers looking to experience the authentic side of Lisbon, there are countless hidden gems, secret viewpoints, local eateries, and off-the-beaten-path activities waiting to be discovered.

Exploring Lesser-Known Neighborhoods

While most visitors stick to the historic city center, these neighborhoods offer a more local and unique experience:

1. Graça: The Authentic Old Lisbon

Located on one of Lisbon's highest hills, Graça offers stunning panoramic views without the crowds of Alfama. This traditional neighborhood is home to Miradouro da Senhora do Monte, one of Lisbon's best-kept secret viewpoints. Here, you can enjoy breathtaking sunsets without the tourist rush. Wander through its narrow streets and experience a slice of authentic Lisbon life with small family-run tascas (local eateries) serving delicious Portuguese food at budget-friendly prices.

2. Campo de Ourique: The Foodie Haven
Campo de Ourique is a charming, residential neighborhood that feels far removed from the tourist-heavy areas. Known for its lively market, Mercado de Campo de Ourique, this district offers a more intimate food scene where you can savor authentic pastéis de nata, gourmet sandwiches, and

fresh seafood. It's also home to some of Lisbon's best bakeries, including Padaria Portuguesa and Aloma, renowned for their award winning custard tarts.

3. Marvila: Lisbon's Hipster District

Once an industrial zone, Marvila has transformed into Lisbon's most up-and-coming neighborhood, filled with creative spaces, trendy cafés, and craft breweries. This area is a paradise for art lovers, with street art murals adorning abandoned warehouses and galleries showcasing the work of local artists. Don't miss Musa, a craft beer brewery offering unique Portuguese-inspired flavors.

Secret Viewpoints & Scenic Spots

Lisbon is famous for its miradouros (viewpoints), but these hidden spots offer a quieter and equally mesmerizing experience:

4. Miradouro de Santo Amaro

Unlike the popular Miradouro de Santa Catarina, this peaceful terrace is a true hidden gem. Located in Alcântara, Miradouro de Santo Amaro provides stunning views of the 25 de Abril Bridge and the Tagus River. It's the perfect spot for a quiet moment of reflection, away from the crowds.

5. Jardim do Torel

A lush garden perched above the city, Jardim do Torel is a beautiful retreat that many tourists overlook. This peaceful oasis offers shaded benches, a small café, and a fantastic view over Avenida da Liberdade. During the summer, the small pond is transformed into a public pool where locals cool off from the Lisbon heat.

Alternative Cultural Experiences

For a deeper understanding of Lisbon's history and culture, venture beyond the typical museums and attractions.

6. Museu da Marioneta (Puppet Museum)

Housed in a former convent, this quirky museum showcases an impressive collection of puppets from around the world. It's an intriguing and unique cultural experience that highlights the artistry behind puppetry and its role in traditional storytelling across different cultures.

7. Thieves Market (Feira da Ladra)

Held every Tuesday and Saturday in Alfama's Campo de Santa Clara, Feira da Ladra is Lisbon's oldest flea market. While tourists flock to Avenida da Liberdade's designer stores, this market offers vintage finds, antiques, handmade crafts, and rare books at bargain prices. It's an excellent place to hunt for unique souvenirs with a local touch.

8. Casa do Alentejo

Hidden behind an unassuming door on Rua das Portas de Santo Antão, Casa do Alentejo is a breathtaking Moorish-style palace that serves as a cultural center for the Alentejo region. Step inside to discover intricate tile work, stunning courtyards, and an affordable restaurant serving traditional Alentejo cuisine.

Local Eateries & Secret Bars

Dining in Lisbon isn't just about well-known restaurants; some of the best meals are found in places only locals know about.

9. Ponto Final

Located across the river in Almada, this waterfront restaurant offers one of the most picturesque dining experiences in Lisbon. A short ferry ride from Cais do Sodré brings you to a peaceful riverside setting where you can enjoy freshly grilled seafood with an unforgettable sunset view.

10. Carvoaria Jacto
For a truly local dining experience, Carvoaria Jacto in the Arroios district is a steakhouse beloved by Lisbon residents. Offering generous portions of perfectly grilled meats at reasonable prices, it's a great alternative to the more touristy steakhouses in the city center.

11. Red Frog Speakeasy
Lisbon has its fair share of stylish bars, but Red Frog is a hidden speakeasy that takes cocktail culture to the next level. Inspired by the Prohibition era, this intimate bar requires a discreet knock on the door for entry. Inside, you'll find expertly crafted cocktails in a cozy, vintage atmosphere.

Unusual Outdoor Adventures
For those looking to explore beyond the city, Lisbon offers plenty of outdoor activities that go beyond traditional sightseeing.

12. Monsanto Forest Park
Often called Lisbon's "green lung," Monsanto Forest Park is the largest urban park in the city, yet it remains relatively unknown to visitors. With hiking trails, picnic spots, and panoramic viewpoints, it's an ideal escape for nature lovers looking to take a break from city life.

13. The Abandoned Panorâmico de Monsanto
Once a luxury restaurant, this abandoned building in Monsanto Forest Park has become one of Lisbon's most intriguing hidden spots. Although officially closed, many urban explorers venture here to see its incredible graffiti-covered walls and spectacular city views.

14. Secret Beaches Near Lisbon

While many tourists visit Cascais for its beaches, locals prefer the quieter, more secluded options just outside the city. Praia da Ursa, located near Cabo da Roca, is a breathtaking and relatively untouched beach with dramatic rock formations. Another great option is Praia da Ribeira do Cavalo, accessible via a scenic hike from Sesimbra.

Unconventional Day Trips

For those looking to venture outside Lisbon, these lesser-known day trips offer unforgettable experiences beyond the usual Sintra and Cascais excursions.

15. Azeitão: Wine & Cheese Paradise

Just 40 minutes from Lisbon, the charming town of Azeitão is famous for its exceptional wines and creamy Azeitão cheese. Visit local wineries like José Maria da Fonseca or Bacalhôa for a wine-tasting experience, and don't forget to try the delicious Tortas de Azeitão, a sweet pastry unique to the region.

16. Berlenga Islands

A hidden paradise off the coast of Peniche, the Berlenga Islands are a protected nature reserve with crystal-clear waters, dramatic cliffs, and historic fortifications. Take a boat from Peniche to explore this untouched gem, perfect for hiking, snorkeling, and spotting marine wildlife.

Chapter 10

Common Tourist Scams & How to Avoid Them

Lisbon is a welcoming and safe city for travelers, but like any popular tourist destination, it has its share of scams and petty crimes. Understanding the most common scams and how to protect yourself will ensure a stress-free and enjoyable trip. Here's a guide to the most frequent tourist scams in Lisbon and how to avoid falling victim to them.

1. Pickpocketing and Bag Snatching

Where it Happens: Crowded tourist areas such as Praça do Comércio, Tram 28, Santa Justa Lift, Rossio Square, metro stations, and busy shopping streets like Rua Augusta.

How it Works: Pickpockets often operate in groups, targeting distracted tourists. They may bump into you, ask for directions, or create distractions while an accomplice steals your belongings. Bag snatching is common in outdoor cafés and public transport.

How to Avoid It:

- Keep valuables in a money belt or an anti-theft backpack with RFID protection.
- Never place your bag on the back of a chair in restaurants or cafés.
- Be cautious when using your phone in public; keep a firm grip on it.
- Avoid keeping wallets in back pockets.

- Stay aware in crowded spaces and watch for unusual behavior.

2. Fake Petition Scam

Where it Happens: Near tourist hotspots like Praça do Comércio, Jerónimos Monastery, and Belém Tower.

How it Works: Scammers, often young individuals, will approach you with a clipboard, claiming to be collecting signatures for a charity or cause. While you are distracted, they or an accomplice will pick your pocket or pressure you into making a donation.

How to Avoid It:

- Politely decline and walk away.
- Do not engage or sign anything.
- Keep valuables secure and be mindful of your surroundings.

3. The Overpriced Tuk-Tuk or Taxi Scam

Where it Happens: Near tourist-heavy areas such as Belém, Alfama, and the airport.

How it Works: Some tuk-tuk drivers and taxi drivers may overcharge tourists by taking longer routes or not using the meter.

How to Avoid It:

- Agree on the price before getting into a tuk-tuk.
- Use ride-hailing apps like Uber or Bolt for fair pricing.
- If taking a taxi, ensure the meter is running or ask for an estimated fare before starting the trip.

4. The Broken ATM/Card Skimming Scam

Where it Happens: ATM machines in less busy streets or near tourist hubs.

How it Works: Some scammers install card skimmers on ATMs to steal your card details. Others may watch you enter your PIN and later attempt to steal your card.

How to Avoid It:

- Use ATMs inside banks rather than on the street.
- Check the card slot for any loose or suspicious attachments.
- Cover the keypad when entering your PIN.
- Monitor your bank statements for any unauthorized transactions.

5. Fake Police Officers

Where it Happens: Near tourist attractions, train stations, or nightlife areas.

How it Works: Scammers impersonating police officers approach tourists and ask to see identification, wallets, or money under the pretense of a "routine check" for counterfeit bills. They then take cash from unsuspecting victims.

How to Avoid It:

- Real police officers in Portugal will never ask for money.
- Ask for their badge and official identification.
- If suspicious, call emergency services (112) and report the incident.

6. Restaurant and Bar Bill Scams

Where it Happens: Restaurants and bars in tourist-heavy locations such as Bairro Alto and Cais do Sodré.

How it Works: Some restaurants charge extra for items you didn't order, add an inflated "tourist tax," or bring appetizers (like bread and olives) and charge exorbitant prices for them.

How to Avoid It:

- Always check the menu for prices before ordering.
- Politely refuse unordered items.
- Examine the bill before paying and question any unexpected charges.
- Stick to well-reviewed restaurants and bars.

7. The 'Helpful' Stranger Scam

Where it Happens: Metro stations, ATMs, and tourist areas.

How it Works: Someone may offer to help with a ticket machine or ATM, only to steal your cash or information. Others might drop something near you and use the distraction to pickpocket you.

How to Avoid It:

- Politely decline assistance from strangers.
- Handle transactions privately.
- Stay vigilant in crowded areas.

8. Cheap Souvenir Scam

Where it Happens: Street markets and souvenir shops in heavily touristed areas like Alfama and Baixa.

How it Works: Some vendors sell counterfeit or low-quality goods, passing them off as authentic Portuguese handicrafts.

How to Avoid It:

- Buy souvenirs from reputable shops or artisans.
- Be wary of deals that seem too good to be true.
- Look for official certification on handcrafted items like azulejos (tiles) and cork products.

9. Fake Charity Collectors

Where it Happens: Busy squares and tourist attractions.

How it Works: Scammers pose as charity workers and pressure tourists into making donations for fictitious causes.

How to Avoid It:

- Do not give money to unverified street charity collectors.
- If interested in donating, research legitimate charities in advance.

10. Free 'Friendship Bracelets' or 'Lucky Charms' Scam

Where it Happens: Rossio Square, Praça do Comércio, and near major landmarks.

How it Works: Scammers approach tourists, offering them a free bracelet or trinket. Once they tie it on your wrist, they demand payment and may become aggressive if refused.

How to Avoid It:

- Do not accept free items from strangers.
- Keep walking and politely decline.

General Safety Tips for Travelers in Lisbon

- Use a Crossbody Bag: Prevents easy snatching and keeps belongings secure.
- Stay Alert in Crowds: Pickpockets target distracted individuals.
- Avoid Flashy Displays of Wealth: Wearing expensive jewelry or showing large amounts of cash can attract scammers.
- Learn Basic Portuguese Phrases: This can help you navigate situations confidently.
- Know Emergency Numbers: The general emergency number in Portugal is 112.

What to Do If You're Scammed

- Report the Incident: Contact the local police or the tourist support line.
- Block Stolen Cards: Contact your bank immediately.
- Seek Assistance: Lisbon's tourist police station in Praça dos Restauradores is available for help.

By staying informed and vigilant, you can fully enjoy Lisbon's vibrant culture, stunning sights, and warm hospitality without worry. With these tips in mind, your trip to Lisbon will be smooth, safe, and scam-free.

Safety Tips for Solo Travelers & Families

Lisbon is known for being one of the safest cities in Europe, with a welcoming atmosphere, friendly locals, and a relatively low crime rate. However, like any major city, travelers should still exercise caution, especially when exploring alone or with family. This chapter provides comprehensive safety tips tailored for solo travelers and families to ensure a secure and enjoyable visit to Portugal's capital.

Safety Tips for Solo Travelers

Traveling alone in Lisbon can be an incredible experience, offering freedom and the chance to immerse yourself in the city's culture at your own pace. However, solo travelers should take extra precautions to stay safe and avoid potential risks.

1. Choose Safe Accommodation

Opt for well-reviewed accommodations in safe neighborhoods like Baixa, Chiado, or Príncipe Real. Read reviews on platforms such as TripAdvisor or Booking.com to ensure the place is secure and has 24-hour reception.

2. Avoid Isolated Areas at Night

While Lisbon is generally safe, some areas can feel deserted at night. Avoid wandering alone in unfamiliar alleyways, particularly in Bairro Alto after bars close or in poorly lit parts of Alfama.

3. Be Cautious with Public Transportation

Lisbon's public transport is efficient and safe, but solo travelers should be mindful of pickpockets on crowded trams, buses, and metro lines. Keep your belongings close and be especially alert on Tram 28, which is known for petty theft.

4. Blend in with the Locals

To avoid unwanted attention, dress modestly and observe how locals behave. Avoid excessive use of maps or phone navigation in public—step inside a café if you need to check directions.

5. Share Your Plans with Someone

Inform a friend or family member about your itinerary, especially if venturing to less touristy areas or taking day trips to places like Sintra or Cascais. Apps like Google Maps allow you to share your real-time location.

6. Stay Aware in Social Settings

If you decide to enjoy Lisbon's vibrant nightlife, be mindful of your drinks and avoid accepting beverages from strangers. Stick to reputable bars and know your way back to your accommodation before heading out.

7. Have Emergency Contacts Ready

Save local emergency numbers in your phone, including Portugal's emergency line (112). If needed, Lisbon has English-speaking police stations, such as the Tourist Police Station near Restauradores Square.

Safety Tips for Families

Traveling with children or elderly family members requires a different approach to safety. Lisbon is a family-friendly city, but parents and guardians should take a few extra steps to ensure a smooth and secure visit.

1. Choose Family-Friendly Accommodation

Look for hotels or rental apartments that cater to families, ideally with child-proofed rooms, on-site dining options, and easy access to public transport. Neighborhoods like Parque das Nações and Estrela are quieter and more suited for families.

2. Plan Your Transportation Wisely

Lisbon's hilly terrain and cobbled streets can be challenging for strollers. If traveling with small children, consider using a baby carrier instead. Public transport is stroller-friendly, but rush hours can be crowded. Taxis and ride-sharing services like Bolt or Uber are convenient alternatives.

3. Keep an Eye on Children in Busy Areas

Popular spots like Praça do Comércio, Belém, and markets such as Time Out Market can get crowded. Establish a meeting point in case family members get separated and consider using ID bracelets for young children with your contact details.

4. Be Prepared for the Sun

Lisbon's summers can be scorching. Carry sunscreen, hats, and refillable water bottles to keep children hydrated. Many parks and squares have shaded areas where families can rest.

5. Teach Children Basic Safety Rules

Before heading out, brief your children on staying close, not talking to strangers, and what to do if they get lost. Many police officers in Lisbon speak English and can assist lost tourists.

6. Watch Out for Tricky Streets

Lisbon's steep streets and trams can be exciting for children but also pose a safety risk. Hold hands when walking on sloped streets and be cautious near tram tracks, as some have little separation from pedestrian areas.

7. Avoid Tourist Scams

Families, especially those with elderly members, should be aware of common scams, such as fake petitions or people posing as charity workers. A firm "no, obrigado" (no, thank you) is usually enough to deter scammers.

Emergency Contacts & Useful Apps

For added security, keep these essential contacts handy:

- Emergency Services (Police, Fire, Ambulance): 112
- Tourist Police (Polícia de Turismo): +351 217 654 242
- Medical Emergency (Hospital Santa Maria): +351 217 805 000
- Lost & Found: +351 213 421 634

- Lisbon Taxi Service: +351 218 119 000

Recommended Apps for Safety & Navigation

- CityMapper: Best for navigating public transport in Lisbon.
- Bolt/Uber: Reliable ride-hailing apps for safer transport.
- Google Translate: Helpful for quick translations.
- Medis: Provides information on nearby pharmacies and medical facilities.

What to Do in an Emergency

While Lisbon is a relatively safe city for tourists, emergencies can happen at any time. Whether dealing with medical issues, lost belongings, or unforeseen incidents, knowing how to respond quickly and effectively is crucial. This guide provides a comprehensive overview of what to do in an emergency while visiting Lisbon.

1. Emergency Contact Numbers in Lisbon

The following emergency numbers can be dialed for immediate assistance:

- 112 – General emergency number for police, fire, and medical services.
- 115 – Fire department (direct contact for non-urgent situations).
- 116 111 – Child helpline for assistance involving minors.
- 808 242 424 – Poison control center.
- 118 – Maritime emergency.

These numbers are toll-free and can be dialed from any phone, including foreign mobile phones.

2. Medical Emergencies

If you or someone you are traveling with experiences a medical emergency, follow these steps:

- Call 112 immediately for an ambulance.
- Provide your location and describe the situation clearly.
- If the emergency is minor, consider going directly to a hospital's Urgência (Emergency Department).
- The main hospitals with 24/7 emergency services include:
  - Hospital de Santa Maria (Avenida Prof. Egas Moniz, 1649-035 Lisboa, +351 217 805 000)
  - Hospital de São José (Rua José António Serrano, 1150-199 Lisboa, +351 218 841 000)
  - CUF Descobertas Hospital (R. Mário Botas 199, 1998-018 Lisboa, +351 210 025 200)

For minor medical concerns, head to a Farmácia (pharmacy), where pharmacists can provide over-the-counter medication and basic medical advice.

3. Reporting a Crime or Theft

Petty crime, such as pickpocketing, can occur in crowded areas like tram stations and tourist sites. If you become a victim of theft or another crime:

- Report it to the nearest Polícia de Segurança Pública (PSP) station.
- The main police station for tourists is:
  o Esquadra de Turismo (Tourist Police Station)
  o Address: Palácio Foz, Praça dos Restauradores, 1250-187 Lisboa
  o Contact: +351 213 421 634
- If your passport is stolen, contact your country's embassy or consulate immediately.
- For stolen credit cards, notify your bank to block your card.

4. Lost or Stolen Passport

If you lose your passport, take the following steps:

- Report the loss at the nearest police station.
- Obtain a Boletim de Ocorrência (police report), which may be required for issuing a replacement passport.
- Visit your embassy or consulate with the police report and any identification documents you have.
- Consider keeping photocopies or digital copies of your passport and travel documents in case of emergencies.

5. Natural Disasters and Environmental Hazards

Lisbon is not prone to extreme natural disasters, but being aware of potential hazards can help you stay safe:

- Earthquakes: Portugal is in a seismic zone. If an earthquake occurs, follow standard safety procedures such as taking cover under sturdy furniture and moving away from windows.
- Wildfires: During the summer, wildfires can break out in rural areas. If traveling outside Lisbon, check local fire warnings and avoid hiking in high-risk zones.
- Extreme Weather: Heavy rainfall can cause localized flooding. Monitor weather alerts if visiting during winter months.

6. Road and Transportation Emergencies

If you experience an emergency while using Lisbon's public transportation or driving:

- Public Transport Issues: If an accident occurs on a tram, metro, or bus, seek assistance from transport staff and call 112 if necessary.
- Taxi or Ride-Sharing Problems: If you feel unsafe in a taxi or ride-sharing vehicle, request to be dropped off in a safe location and report the issue to the respective service provider.
- Car Accidents: Call 112 for police and medical assistance. If the accident is minor, exchange details with the other driver and file a report with local authorities.

7. Financial Emergencies

If you lose your wallet or run out of money while in Lisbon:

- Contact Your Bank: Most international banks have emergency services to block stolen cards and issue replacements.
- Western Union or MoneyGram: Use these services to receive emergency funds from family or friends.
- Visit Your Embassy: Some embassies may offer assistance for stranded travelers.

8. Personal Safety Tips to Prevent Emergencies

Being proactive can help you avoid emergencies before they happen:

- Keep your belongings secure and avoid carrying large amounts of cash.
- Use ATMs in well-lit areas and be cautious of skimming devices.
- Stay aware of your surroundings, especially in crowded areas.
- Learn a few basic Portuguese phrases to communicate in case of an emergency.
- Purchase travel insurance that covers medical expenses, theft, and trip cancellations.

9. Emergency Resources & Useful Apps

Downloading useful apps can help you stay informed and prepared:

- 112 SOS App – Directly contacts emergency services with GPS location.
- Google Translate – Helps with language barriers.
- Metro Lisboa App – Provides real-time metro updates.
- Uber/Bolt – Alternative transportation in case of emergencies.

- Embassy Locator – Helps locate your nearest embassy or consulate.

Chapter 11

Tips from Locals & Experienced Travelers

A local's guide to Lisbon: 10 top tips

The Serbian-born writer picks the best places in his 'beautiful, luminous' adopted city for eating, shopping, walking or just hanging out and soaking up the views

Before I moved to Lisbon, almost a quarter of a century ago, someone told me: "From afar, it looks like a queen. But from closer you see that the old empress's make-up is smudged and flaking, and that the ornaments fluttering in the wind are not lace, but someone's laundry drying at the windows. But she's still is a real beauty."

I fell in love with Lisbon from the off. The city has since been seriously spruced up and redeveloped, but it hasn't lost its shabby-chic glamour. It's a very user-friendly city: not too big, not too small, safe, and not too expensive. Even today, 20 years later, it still manages to surprise me with its beauty and luminosity.

Terreiro do Paço

Praça do Comércio is a large square flanked by elegant buildings, with one side open to the river Tagus, or Tejo in Portuguese. Lisboans still call it by its old name, Terreiro do Paço, or Palace Courtyard. It was the emblematic centre of the Portuguese empire, where kings lived, and precious spices and colonial goods were traded for gold. In 1755,

Lisbon was hit by a huge earthquake, followed by a fire and a tsunami, which almost destroyed it in a day. The square in its present incarnation rose from the rubble of that disaster. It was also here that, in 1974, a military coup turned into a popular democracy movement, with red carnations in the barrels of the soldiers' rifles. It is a good starting point for exploring Lisbon on hop-on-hop-off double-decker buses.

Bistro 100 Maneiras
This is a story of unforeseen success. The owner, Ljubomir Stanisic, born in Sarajevo, fled the war to Portugal as a boy. Now he is a celebrity chef, with books, his own TV programme, and restaurants that are the height of fashion. Bistro 100 Maneiras, a two-floor restaurant in an art deco mansion in the busy Bairro Alto district, is perfect for high-end dining: squid, octopus, rack of lamb. The space is elegant yet informal, there's a refined selection of cocktails and the best Portuguese wines, and each dish is a wonderful surprise. You can dine here for €40 a head.
Largo da Trindade 9, 100maneiras.com, open Sun–Sat 7pm–2am

Miradouro da Graça

Lisbon's climate means that, with a bit of luck, we can be outdoors all year round. The city's *miradouros*, or viewpoints, are perfect spots to hang out. Miradouro da Graça is my favourite. On a terrace high above Lisbon's patchwork of tiled roofs, in the shadow of pine trees, you can enjoy the breeze while sipping a coffee or cold beer. Downtown, the medieval castle, the red suspension bridge, the river, and the statue of Christ, arms wide open overlooking the estuary, all fit into a single fascinating picture, and it's especially photogenic at sunset.

The city on seven hills also offers many other panoramic views. Santa Catarina, Senhora do Monte, Monte Agudo ... Any place called a miradouro is an excellent place to chill. And pay attention to the sky: here it is two tones closer to indigo than the regular sky blue. You will be surprised by the whiteness of clouds against that blue.

Calçada da Graça

Casa Independente

Intendente is the most diverse and multicultural area in Portugal. Once a druggy red light district, it has been taken over by hipsters, immigrants and artists. Intendente square proper is encircled by historic buildings – some restored, some not – and small bars serving *petiscos* (similar to tapas) at pavement tables. It is a lovely, friendly place to linger from morning till late at night, over a small draft beer (€2).

Inside the 17th-century palace that dominates the square is Casa Independente Cultural Association, founded five years ago. It's a wonderful alternative space, with high-ceilinged lounges, scruffy back garden and enormous ballroom. I like its relaxed atmosphere, petiscos, and eclectic cultural and musical programme.

Take the tram to **the Thieves' M**arket

Do a classic Lisbon city-safari by taking the number 28 tram, which passes through the popular districts of Graça, Alfama, Baixa and Estrela. The trams are small, like wardrobes on wheels, to pass through the narrow streets of the oldest quarters. For many years, on Saturday mornings, I have been taking the 28 through the labyrinth of Alfama to Feira da Ladra, or Thieves' Market. It is an open-air flea market overlooking the river: picturesque, colourful, swarming with people, yet surprisingly calm, where you can stroll, buy trinkets (cash only), and have lunch. It's full of amazing things, from authentic antiques to authentic trash.

Campo de Santa Clara, Tue & Sat, 9am–2pm

'Typical' restaurants
Portuguese cuisine is simple and honest. The fish is fresh from the ocean, the steaks juicy, the wine full-bodied. Lisbon's old-school *restaurantes tipicos*, are easy to recognise, with meat and fish on ice, and paper tablecloths. My three favourites have become so popular I have to book, or even queue. They're all in the same neighbourhood, so if I don't get a table in one, I try another.

For the most exquisite grilled cod or octopus in green olive oil, go to Cova Funda, just off Intendente square; for the freshest shellfish, there's Marisqueira Lis, just across the avenue; and for a charcoal grill, the Carvoaria Jacto steakhouse, two blocks away (the owner is a butcher, so he knows his meat). Whichever you choose, you'll wine and dine well for under €20.

Take a walking tour

For several years now, a group of young people calling themselves the Lisbon Walkers have been taking locals and tourists on guided walking tour. It's a lovely way to experience Lisbon. For beginners, there is a general tour, but things get more exciting when you choose to see Lisbon district by district. There are also special interest tours: medieval, African, Jewish, freemason, literary or underground Lisbon. My favourite tour is on legends and mysteries: two hours learning about Ulysses as the founder of Lisbon, the young martyrs of Lisbon and St Vincent and the ravens, for €15.

Daily tours in English start from the meeting point in Terreiro do Paço, lisbonwalker.com

National Coach Museum

The collection of royal vehicles at the Museu Nacional dos Coches in Belem transports you back in time. The oldest vehicle, from 1619, brought Philip III of Spain to Lisbon to take over the throne; the last to be used drove a young Queen Elizabeth II to visit the Portuguese dictator Antonio Salazar in 1957. A trio of opulent coaches were made in 1716 and sent to Rome by the richest of all the kings of Portugal, João V "the Pious", to show to the Pope how devout he was and how prosperous his empire. For a taste of Lisbon at the height of the inquisition, I recommend the novel Baltasar and Blimunda, by the Portuguese Nobel prize laureate José Saramago. It's a story of love, miracles and flying machines.

Avenida da Índia 136, €8, closed Monday

Lisbon Oceanarium

Oceanário de Lisboa is perfect for a rainy day. It's home to water creatures of all kinds, shapes and sizes: colourful anemones and corals, sea-stars, fluorescent jellyfish, dragonfish, exotic frogs, penguins and playful sea otters. In the massive circular central glass tank swim large fish, such as sunfish, manta rays and sharks. It is in the hyper-modern

Parque das Nações, the suburb built from scratch on the waterfront for Expo 1998, by the futuristic Gare do Oriente station.

Open 10am–7pm, adult 16,20, child €10.80, buy tickets online to avoid queueing

Estoril

Sunbathing on Tamariz beach with Estoril Castle in the background.

Thirty minutes west of the city, the seaside resort of Estoril, with its Grand Casino, was founded in 1935 – for the amusement of Lisbon's rich. At the beginning of the second world war, Lisbon was an important escape route from Europe, and nearby Estoril unexpectedly became an international destination for refugees. Its Hotel Palácio sheltered the likes of Salvador Dalí, Antoine du Saint-Exupéry, Ian Fleming, and the Duke and of Windsor and Wallis Simpson. As well as a lot of spies.

After the war the resort became a haven for exiled monarchs and dictators, who used to meet in the Palácio for Sunday lunch. Later, it became popular among celebrities, including Orson Welles, Gina Lollobrigida, Sophia Loren, Luchino Visconti and Zsa Zsa Gabor. Rooms in the Palácio, which is as elegant and pompous as ever, still carry their names. Some years ago, it was reported that restoration work in the hotel had uncovered kilometres of wiring left over from war espionage.

Today, Estoril is a quiet, wealthy seaside town with subtropical vegetation, golf courses and sandy beaches. It's ideal for a day trip.

Trains from Lisbon's Cais do Sodré station depart every 30 minutes, €2.25 one way

Dejan Tiago-Stanković's debut novel, Estoril is published by Head of Zeus, £12.99. To buy a copy for £11.04 with free UK p&p, go to guardianbookshop.com

Way to go

Flights
Easyjet and Ryanair fly to Lisbon from several UK cities from £82 return.

Where to stay
In a classic early 20th-century building with tiled facade and wrought iron balcony, B&B Casa Amora (doubles from €115) is named after a Portuguese artist and has a sunny patio for breakfast or afternoon drinks.

Best time to go
April-May and September-October: prices are lower but weather can still be beach-friendly.

Exchange rate £1 = €1.15

A small beer in a neighbourhood bar costs from €1.80, a coffee about €1.

Best-kept Secrets only Locals Know

Lisbon is one of the oldest cities in Europe, enjoying a rich culture full of soulful music, unique artistry, and mouthwatering food – not to mention the spectacular views. So it's no surprise that the city receives over one million visitors every year.

But while most of those visitors will spend their time battling the crowds at popular tourist attractions like Belém Tower, the Jeronimos Monastery, and the Castelo de S. Jorge, there are a lot more hidden gems in Lisbon than what you'd think – you just need to make it up the hills first.

Here's a list of some of our favourite hidden gems we found while exploring the city of seven hills.

1. The winding streets of the Alfama Quarter

The oldest and most unique quarter in Lisbon, Alfama is a maze of winding streets and colourful alleys. Built sometime around the 8th century by the Moors, and later occupied by the Romans, visiting Alfama is like stepping back in time. It's an area unlike any other in Lisbon, having survived a catastrophic earthquake in 1755, which destroyed over half of the city. Wandering the narrow streets, you will find hidden terraces with unique views of the port and terracotta rooftops with some great examples of Portugal's famous Tiles.

Exploring the quarter at night, you will also be treated to the sounds of traditional Fado music, which was created in 1870 right in the heart of Alfama. The word 'Fado' translates to fate and involves a sorrowful solo singer accompanied by a lone classical Portuguese guitar. It's often performed in small restaurants, bars, and Fado Houses in Alfama and Bairro Alto and is a bucket list item for anyone visiting Lisbon.

Spend a day exploring the tight-knit streets and lookouts throughout the old town before sitting down for a meal or drink while you're entertained with a traditional Fado performance at underrated local Alfama restaurants like Fado Na Morgadinha or Tasca Do Chico.

2. Hotel Mundial rooftop bar

With its sunny blue skies and colourful buildings, there's no question that Lisbon is a city worth photographing. And while the views from Alfama and the Castelo de S. Jorge are lovely, we've found an even more unique view worth capturing – plus this one comes with a drink!

Every recommendation list needs at least one rooftop bar, and this truly is one of the hidden gems in Lisbon. The Hotel Mundial in Baixa sits in the heart of Lisbon, and is one of the tallest buildings in the area. This means great views, especially from their lush rooftop bar and lounge. The large terrace is open to the public and offers unbeatable panoramic sights of the city and port. Best of all, the bar is open – so grab a seat and a cocktail and enjoy the view. I'd definitely recommend timing it so that you get here an hour or so before sunset for those golden hour photos.

3. Time out market

Lisbon offers no shortage of options when it comes to food, but if you're looking to try the best of the best, and want a range of options, a visit to Time Out Market needs to be on your itinerary.

Owned and operated by Time Out Magazine, this food hall is a unique take on a familiar concept. Time Out Market is one of the largest gourmet food locations in the world, with spaces rented out to various restaurants, bars, and specialty shops for anywhere from one week to three years. Only the best of the best is allowed, with everything tested for excellence by an independent panel of city experts.

In Time Out's own words "if it's good it goes into the magazine, if it's great it goes into the market".

With 26 restaurants boasting both traditional and foreign cuisines, 8 bars, a dozen specialty shops, and even a music venue, the atmosphere in the food hall is buzzing, and there's no shame in going back two or three times to try the different foods on offer. Just make sure to leave some room to sample a few of the delicious desserts scattered around the hall.

Pro tip: stop by Manteigaria on your way out to pick up one – or three, no judgment here! – of their flaky, golden pastel de natas for the journey home.

4. Fronteira Palace

Conveniently located within city limits, the Palácio de Fronteira is a treat for both history buffs and architecture lovers. And even if history and architecture aren't really your things, it's hard not to be impressed by the lush gardens, ornate fountains, and gorgeous rooms.

Built in the 17th century and originally used as a hunting lodge and secondary residence to the influential Mascarenhas family, Fronteira Palace is a unique piece of history and is still the official residence of the Marqueses de Fronteira. With some of the best examples of traditional Portuguese tiles combined with Italian baroque architecture, the palace gardens and halls are worth a visit.

The picture-worthy gardens are open to the public and feature winding hedge gardens, tiled walls and alcoves, and many statues and busts. Another one of our hidden gems in Lisbon, this site is much quieter than other Lisbon attractions, and if you're lucky you might even have the gardens all to yourself. And if you're looking for a more in-depth understanding of the palace you can also book a guided tour inside where you can learn more about the history and view the 17th century antiques and tilework.

5. Dear Breakfast, Alfama

Pancakes are a surprisingly popular breakfast option in Portugal – usually served with a fried egg, bacon, and a little bit of greens on the side. Being a big fan of pancakes myself, it's safe to say I ate more than my fair share in Lisbon, the tastiest of which were from this absolute gem of a cafe – Dear Breakfast.

A bustling all-day breakfast cafe, Dear Breakfast has three locations in Lisbon and offers good vibes and instagram-worthy food. The Alfama location features concrete floors, vaulted brick ceilings, and enough tropical plants to give it a calming bohemian vibe. The ingredients are all locally sourced and they pride themselves on the quality of their dishes, particularly the eggs.

This is a great brunch option, but make sure you book in advance, as it can get pretty busy in the morning – food this good won't stay a secret forever.

6. Estufa Fria Botanical Garden

While Lisbon is a city of tightly packed streets and seemingly endless stairs and hills, there are still a few places where you can escape into nature. One such escape, and one of our hidden gems in Lisbon, is the Estufa Fria Botanical Gardens, an accidental garden turned oasis.

Once an abandoned and barren Basalt Quarry, in the early 1900s a local gardener began using the space to temporarily shelter his exotic plant collection. However, World War One forced him to abandon his project and plants to the quarry. However, the plants didn't die and instead actually thrived, and it was found that the quarry was an ideal environment for a garden, becoming an official Greenhouse in 1933.

Estufa Fria (or Cold Greenhouse in English) is now a thriving garden with over 300 plant species, scattered with small waterfalls, hidden caves, and lakes. It is one of the largest cold greenhouses in the world and uses a natural heating system. The site also includes two other greenhouses that you can visit, the Hot Greenhouse, which houses tropical plants, and the Sweet Greenhouse for succulents.

With over 3.7 acres to explore, Estufa Fria is an excellent way to escape from the city for a few hours.

7. Ponto Final

A little bit off the beaten track – or over the Ponto 25 de Abril bridge in this case – is a restaurant where you can dine right on the water. If you're looking for an unbeatable view of Lisbon to enjoy with your lunch or dinner this is it.

Located in Almada, Ponto Final is a traditional Portuguese restaurant that you'll either need to get a taxi or board a ferry to from central Lisbon. But the unique views are well worth it, and if you can score a table outside on the jetty, the experience is well worth it. This is your chance to enjoy a traditional steak or seafood dish with a glass of wine while you sit gazing out at the Tagu river and impressive red bridge. Try to book a table in advance if you can, as the restaurant is popular among locals and it may be a long wait otherwise.

8. Castle of the Moors & Monserrate Palace, Sintra

A visit to Lisbon wouldn't be complete without a day trip out to Sintra, a picturesque Portuguese town, UNESCO World Heritage site, and former summer retreat for royalty and nobility. Sintra itself isn't much of a secret and is popular among tourists, however, most people find their way to the colourful Pena Palace and gardens, which is impressive if a little bit over-hyped.

Personally, my favourite place in Sintra has to be the Castle of the Moors. Looking like something out of a fairytale and with views of the Atlantic Ocean, this fortress was built in the 8th century by the Moors and was an important player in the defense of Sintra and the ports of Lisbon during Moorish and later Portuguese rule. The Castle has been largely destroyed over time, but the chapel and impressive fortress walls still stand, giving you the unique opportunity to explore a genuine medieval fort – with the best views in all of Sintra.

Another of Sintra's hidden gems, which is definitely worth the visit, is Monserrate Palace. Built on the ruins of the former palace in the 19th century, this is one of the best examples of Romantic architecture in Portugal. The unique mix of Medieval and Eastern decorations set against the background of Monserrate's exotic gardens feels like something out of a movie. And with smaller crowds, exploring the palace and gardens can be a magical experience.

Lisbon is a city teeming withgood food, good weather, and beautiful architecture. And with buildings that date back to the 8th century and a rich history to discover there's truly something for everyone. So take a step off the tourist track and experience some of the truly unique things that Lisbon has to offer.

If Lisbon or Portugal is next on your bucket list, check out our <u>Contiki Portugal trips</u>. On Contiki you can visit some of the most iconic and stunning destinations in Portugal, and experience the best this sunny country has to offer, plus our expert Trip Managers will share all their best Portugal hidden gems with you!

BONUS SECTIONS

ITINERARIES

Ultimate 7-Day Lisbon Itinerary

This seven-day itinerary is designed to help you explore Lisbon's iconic sights, cultural experiences, and hidden gems while balancing sightseeing, relaxation, and culinary delights.

Day 1: Introduction to Lisbon – Historic Core & Landmarks

Morning:

- **Breakfast at Café A Brasileira** – Start your day at one of Lisbon's oldest cafés in Chiado. Try a strong Portuguese espresso and a pastel de nata.
- **Praça do Comércio & Rua Augusta Arch** – Walk through Lisbon's grandest square and climb to the top of the arch for panoramic views.
- **Alfama & Miradouros** – Wander through Lisbon's oldest neighborhood, stopping at Miradouro de Santa Luzia and Miradouro das Portas do Sol for breathtaking city views.

Afternoon:

- **São Jorge Castle** – Explore the historic fortress that overlooks Lisbon. Enjoy stunning vistas from the castle walls.

- **Lunch at Chapitô à Mesa** – A restaurant with a spectacular view of the city and a creative atmosphere.
- **Lisbon Cathedral (Sé de Lisboa)** – Visit the city's iconic cathedral, a mix of Romanesque and Gothic architecture.

Evening:

- **Dinner in Alfama & Fado Experience** – Head to a traditional Fado house like Clube de Fado for an authentic Portuguese music performance with dinner.

Day 2: Belem – Lisbon's Age of Discovery

Morning:

- **Breakfast at Pastéis de Belém** – Try the world-famous custard tarts at their original home.
- **Jerónimos Monastery** – Visit this UNESCO-listed masterpiece of Manueline architecture.
- **Belém Tower & Monument to the Discoveries** – Walk along the Tagus River and explore these iconic landmarks.

Afternoon:

- **Lunch at Pão Pão Queijo Queijo** – A budget-friendly spot for sandwiches and Portuguese-style snacks.
- **MAAT (Museum of Art, Architecture, and Technology)** – A modern architectural wonder with fascinating exhibitions.

251

Evening:

- **Sunset at LX Factory** – Enjoy dinner and drinks at this trendy creative hub with street art, shops, and rooftop bars.

Day 3: Modern Lisbon & Cultural Spots

Morning:

- **Breakfast at Fabrica Coffee Roasters** – One of the best coffee spots in Lisbon.
- **Parque das Nações** – Visit the futuristic side of Lisbon, home to **Oceanário de Lisboa**, one of Europe's largest aquariums.

Afternoon:

- **Lunch at Honorato Hamburgueres Artesanais** – Great for gourmet burgers.
- **Calouste Gulbenkian Museum** – A hidden gem showcasing an incredible private art collection.

Evening:

- **Dinner at Bairro do Avillez** – A top-notch restaurant by celebrity chef José Avillez.
- **Night Out in Príncipe Real** – Discover Lisbon's trendiest bars, such as Gin Lovers & Less or Pavilhão Chinês.

Day 4: Sintra Day Trip – Fairytale Palaces & Forests

Morning:

- **Early Train to Sintra (40 min from Lisbon)**
- **Pena Palace & Park** – Visit this colorful mountaintop palace, one of Portugal's most stunning sights.

Afternoon:

- **Lunch in Sintra** – Try Tascantiga, a cozy spot with delicious petiscos (Portuguese tapas).
- **Quinta da Regaleira** – Explore the magical gardens and mysterious underground tunnels.
- **Moorish Castle** – Hike to the ancient fortress ruins for breathtaking views.

Evening:

- **Dinner at Cantinho do Avillez in Lisbon** – Relax after a long day with a refined yet cozy meal.

Day 5: Day Trip to Cascais & Coastal Beauty

Morning:

- **Train to Cascais (40 min from Lisbon)**
- **Wander through Cascais Old Town** – Stroll past charming streets, historic buildings, and oceanfront scenery.

Afternoon:

- **Lunch at Mar do Inferno** – A seafood restaurant with fresh local catches.

- **Boca do Inferno & Guincho Beach** – Visit these dramatic cliffs and then relax on one of Portugal's best beaches.

Evening:

- **Return to Lisbon & Dinner at Ramiro** – Enjoy the city's best seafood, including the famous garlic shrimp and seafood rice.

Day 6: Off-the-Beaten-Path Lisbon

Morning:

- **Brunch at Heim Café** – A cozy spot for delicious pancakes and coffee.
- **LX Factory & Village Underground** – Explore Lisbon's artistic and cultural hubs filled with street art and unique shops.

Afternoon:

- **Lunch at O Frade** – A hidden gem serving authentic Alentejan cuisine.
- **Tapada das Necessidades Park** – A peaceful retreat away from the crowds.

Evening:

- **Dinner at Taberna da Rua das Flores** – An intimate eatery with ever-changing dishes.
- **Rooftop Drinks at PARK Bar** – A perfect way to end the night with sunset views.

Day 7: Relaxation & Last Explorations

Morning:

- **Breakfast at Manteigaria** – Another contender for the best pastel de nata.
- **Tile Workshop or Shopping for Souvenirs** – Visit Cortiço & Netos for traditional azulejos.

Afternoon:

- **Lunch at Mercado de Campo de Ourique** – A lesser-known food market with excellent local eats.
- **Ride Tram 28 One Last Time** – Enjoy a scenic route through Lisbon's most iconic neighborhoods.

Evening:

- **Farewell Dinner at Solar dos Presuntos** – End your trip with a classic Portuguese feast.

PHRASES IN PORTUGUESE

Here are **30 essential Portuguese phrases and vocabulary** that travelers should learn before visiting Lisbon. These will help with greetings, ordering food, asking for directions, and other common travel situations.

Basic Greetings & Politeness

1. **Olá** – Hello
2. **Bom dia** – Good morning
3. **Boa tarde** – Good afternoon
4. **Boa noite** – Good evening / Good night
5. **Adeus** – Goodbye
6. **Até logo** – See you later
7. **Por favor** – Please
8. **Obrigado** (if you're male) / **Obrigada** (if you're female) – Thank you
9. **De nada** – You're welcome
10. **Desculpe** – Excuse me / I'm sorry

Asking for Help & Directions

11. **Fala inglês?** – Do you speak English?
12. **Não falo português muito bem.** – I don't speak Portuguese very well.
13. **Pode ajudar-me?** – Can you help me?
14. **Onde fica...?** – Where is...?
15. **Como posso chegar a...?** – How can I get to...?
16. **À direita** – To the right
17. **À esquerda** – To the left
18. **Em frente** – Straight ahead

Perto / Longe – Near / Far

19. **Quanto custa?** – How much does it cost?

At a Restaurant or Café

21. **A ementa, por favor.** – The menu, please.
22. **O que recomenda?** – What do you recommend?
23. **Eu gostaria de...** – I would like...
24. **A conta, por favor.** – The bill, please.
25. **Com licença, pode trazer mais água?** – Excuse me, can you bring more water?
26. **Está delicioso!** – It's delicious!

Transportation & Accommodation

27. **Onde fica a estação de metro mais próxima?** – Where is the nearest metro station?
28. **Preciso de um táxi.** – I need a taxi.
29. **Tenho uma reserva.** – I have a reservation.
30. **A que horas é o check-out?** – What time is check-out?

CONCLUSION

Conclusion: The Ultimate Lisbon Travel Experience

Lisbon is a city of contrasts—where ancient traditions blend seamlessly with modern culture, where cobbled streets lead to breathtaking viewpoints, and where every meal tells a story of Portugal's rich culinary heritage. Whether you are drawn to its historic landmarks, vibrant nightlife, stunning coastline, or charming neighborhoods, Lisbon offers a travel experience that is both dynamic and unforgettable.

This guide has taken you through every aspect of planning a trip to Lisbon, from essential travel information to detailed itineraries, hidden gems, and practical tips for making the most of your stay. As we conclude, let's reflect on what makes Lisbon truly special and why it continues to captivate travelers from all around the world.

A City of History, Culture, and Timeless Beauty

Lisbon is one of Europe's oldest capitals, with a history dating back thousands of years. The city's past is evident in its stunning architecture, from the Moorish influences in Alfama to the grand Manueline style of Jerónimos Monastery. Walking through the city feels like stepping back in time, yet Lisbon is anything but frozen in history.

The city has reinvented itself over the centuries, evolving into a thriving metropolis with a contemporary edge. The revitalization of neighborhoods like LX Factory and the rise of rooftop bars and creative hubs have given Lisbon a fresh and youthful energy while maintaining its deep cultural roots.

For travelers, this blend of old and new creates an experience that is constantly engaging. Whether you are exploring ancient castles, visiting world-class museums, or simply watching the sunset over the Tagus River, Lisbon offers a journey through time that is both immersive and rewarding.

A Culinary Haven for Food Lovers

One of the undeniable highlights of any trip to Lisbon is its **food scene**. From humble pastelarias serving the iconic **pastel de nata** to Michelin-starred restaurants pushing the boundaries of Portuguese cuisine, Lisbon caters to every palate.

The city's markets, such as **Time Out Market** and **Mercado de Campo de Ourique**, showcase Portugal's finest ingredients, while family-run taverns serve **bacalhau** in all its delicious variations. The rich flavors of Portuguese seafood, the warmth of a traditional Fado restaurant, and the simple pleasure of enjoying a bifana sandwich with a cold beer are all part of what makes Lisbon a food lover's paradise.

For those looking to dive deeper, wine tastings, cooking classes, and food tours provide an even greater appreciation of Portugal's gastronomic traditions. Lisbon doesn't just feed the stomach—it feeds the soul.

Unforgettable Experiences and Unique Attractions

Lisbon is not just about sightseeing; it's about experiences that stay with you long after you leave. Some of the city's best moments are the **simple joys** of everyday life—riding the iconic **Tram 28**, listening to the melancholic sounds of

Fado in a dimly lit tavern, or sipping a ginjinha on a street corner with friendly locals.

The city's location also makes it a **perfect base** for exploring beyond its borders. A day trip to **Sintra** unveils fairytale palaces, mystical gardens, and breathtaking landscapes, while **Cascais** and **Costa da Caparica** offer sun-drenched beaches and scenic coastal views. The **Arrábida Natural Park** is a paradise for nature lovers, with its crystal-clear waters and lush hiking trails.

Lisbon is also a city that embraces its creative side. Whether it's street art in **Bairro Alto**, the contemporary exhibitions at **MAAT**, or the vibrant nightlife in **Pink Street**, there's always something happening in Lisbon. It's a city that inspires, surprises, and invites exploration at every turn.

A City That Feels Like Home

One of the most beautiful aspects of Lisbon is the warmth of its people. **Portuguese hospitality** is famous for its authenticity, and Lisbon is no exception. The locals, known as **Lisboetas**, are welcoming, friendly, and always ready to share a recommendation or a story about their city. Even if you only learn a few words of Portuguese, you'll find that small efforts go a long way in making connections.

Lisbon is a city that makes you feel at home, whether you're wandering through a lively market, chatting with an old shopkeeper, or simply watching the world go by from a riverside café.

Practical Tips for an Amazing Lisbon Trip

To make the most of your trip to Lisbon, keep these key takeaways in mind:

1. **Best Time to Visit:** Spring (March-May) and Autumn (September-November) offer the best weather and fewer crowds. Summer is vibrant but can be hot and busy.
2. **Getting Around:** Walking is the best way to explore, but Lisbon's public transport—trams, metro, buses, and ferries—makes getting around easy.
3. **Budgeting:** Lisbon can be an affordable destination if you take advantage of **budget-friendly eats, free attractions, and happy hour deals**.
4. **Cultural Etiquette:** Portuguese people value politeness, so a simple "obrigado" (thank you) goes a long way.
5. **Safety:** Lisbon is a safe city, but be mindful of pickpockets in crowded areas.
6. **Local Insights:** Venture beyond the tourist hotspots—some of Lisbon's best experiences lie in **hidden alleyways, lesser-known miradouros, and tiny neighborhood eateries**.

Why You'll Want to Return to Lisbon

Lisbon is the kind of city that **leaves a lasting impression**. Its combination of history, culture, and modern vibrancy makes it one of the most captivating destinations in the world. Whether it's your first visit or your tenth, Lisbon always has something new to offer.

Perhaps it's the light that paints the city golden in the late afternoon, the sound of seagulls echoing through the streets, or the taste of a perfectly crisp pastel de nata. Maybe it's the friendliness of the locals, the smell of grilled sardines in the summer, or the feeling of standing atop a miradouro and seeing the city stretch out before you.

Whatever it is, Lisbon has a way of **calling travelers back.**

As you close this guide and prepare for your journey, remember that Lisbon is best experienced **with curiosity, an open heart, and a sense of adventure.** Let yourself wander, discover, and fall in love with the city's charm.

Your Lisbon adventure is waiting—**boa viagem!**

Made in United States
North Haven, CT
13 July 2025

70662369R00143